MELISSA ETHERIDGE lives in Southern California. Visit the Melissa Etheridge Information Network at www.melissaetheridge.com

LAURA MORTON has co-authored a number of bestselling celebrity books. She lives in New York City.

D0061794

The Truth Is...

My Life in Love and Music

...

Melissa Etheridge

with Laura Morton

RANDOM HOUSE TRADE PAPERBACKS

New York

RANDOM HOUSE TRADE PAPERBACKS and colophon are trademarks of
Random House, Inc.

This work was originally published in hardcover in
a slightly different form by Villard Books in 2001.

Except where otherwise credited, photographs and other material appear-
ing in this book are from the personal collection of Melissa Etheridge.

Song lyric credits are located on page 238.

LIBRARY OF CONGRESS CATALOGING-IN-PUBLICATION DATA
Etheridge, Melissa.
    The truth is . . .: my life in love and music / Melissa Etheridge with
Laura Morton.
        p. cm.
    ISBN 0-375-76026-1
    1. Etheridge, Melissa. 2. Rock musicians—Biography. I. Morton,
Laura. II. Title.
ML420.E88 A3   2001
782.42166′092—dc21   2001023733
    [B]

Random House website address: www.atrandom.com

Printed in the United States of America on acid-free paper

98765432

First Trade Paperback Edition

Dedicated in truth to Beckett and Bailey
with every last drop of love inside of me.
With Love,
Your Mama

My understanding of truth can change from day to day
And my commitment must be to truth rather than to consistency.

—Ram Dass

Acknowledgments

...

I would like to thank you, dear reader, for taking this time, right now, to take in some of the pieces of my life. That is all this is, you know, just pieces, bits of what I remember and how I remember them.

I thank my mother for her ability to change and for standing by me even when what I speak and write might be painful for her.

I thank my manager, Bill, for believing in every single thing I have ever done and finding a way to let me do it.

Thank you Laura Morton for being a sounding board, therapist, friend, and writer, at a time in my life when everything was new and examining the old gave me strength. You were right, I could have it.

Thank you Alex Metcalf, for helping to bring this book to fruition. You are my true friend forever . . . and damn talented, and a great husband and father, and sexy too, but what do I know?

Thank you Bruce Tracy at Villard for not falling apart under deadlines and clearing the space to let me do this.

There have been so many people in my life, some mentioned here, most, not. I thank you for the experience of knowing you, your hard work, your friendship, and your time. I am merely at the middle of this journey. Let me tell you about it, the truth . . .

—M.E.

Contents

...

Introduction	xiii
Lonely Is a Child	3
Ready to Love	25
I Don't Think We're in Kansas Anymore	41
Home Again	49
Los Angeles	57
Bring Me Some Water	71
'Oh My God, That's Me'	93
Julie	105
Brave and Crazy	117
Talking to My Angel	125
Yes I Am	131
Your Little Secret	149
Pregnancy	157
Mothering	167
Breakdown	181
Lover Please	187
The End	201
Skin	209
The Beginning	219
Afterword	232

Introduction

...

July 8, 1975, age 14

To Myself:

Who are you? Where are you?

Why do you hide so?

I search for you, for an answer.

But I always end with a handful of broken dreams.

An old tattered heart

Worn down over the years.

Inside of you is the pain and the sorrow you dare not let show,

for fear that other minds might think that you are really reaching

for someone who might understand.

Your heart is heavy, for it holds the tears.

But I should have cried, "come out!"

Come out of that dark shell you hide in.

If they only knew that for every time I've laughed,

I have shed a tear.

Am I so afraid of you that I cannot stand face to face with you?

Yes.

I fear you more than the darkest night.

For I share the deep sorrow you feel.

You are part of me—the part no one has seen.

You are behind this mask I wear.

When I am alone, you make me see what I really am.

And I cry.

If only I could set you free.

Let you live the life I long for.

But I shall move on. Taking life with a smile and you shall take
    the pain.

And I will never cry.

For those who cry feel sadness.

And I am not sad

Or am I?

—Missy Etheridge

OH, THE PAIN. READING THIS AGAIN, I CAN STILL FEEL THE
pain all of these years later. I suppose that I was suffering from regular everyday teenage angst, but it felt like so much more back then.

I've always been good at chronicling the many moods of my
life, but mostly I have done it through my music. I tell stories of
life, pain, joy, and love in three-minute snippets—little glimpses of
who I am or who people perceive me to be. What I really am is this
little girl looking for acceptance. Looking for love and trying to fill
up this hole inside of me that has always been empty. Big-time
empty.

This is the story of my truth. What you are about to read is
my perception of the events that have shaped my life, inspired my
music, and brought me to a new understanding of myself and my
life. I don't really think of it as my life story; rather it's the stories
that have made up the layers of my first forty years. Sometimes, I
think it would be a lot easier, and less energy would be expended,
to not live so rooted in my truth. But the truth is always better. People may disagree, and some may not like what I have to say, but I

stand by my truth. You see, my truth can sometimes collide with someone else's truth. That doesn't make my version more important. Nor does it diminish the significance each version brings to our lives. It's simply the difference between how I remember things versus how somebody else might remember the same things.

When I first sat down to write this book, I had no particular plan to pursue another concert tour in the foreseeable future, if at all. There was no real thought of writing any new songs, let alone cutting a seventh album. I wanted to spend more time at home with my family—watch my kids grow up, and spend quality time with my partner. At that time, *that* was my truth. Here it is, one year later, and though I have completed my book, I have also composed a new album, and I am getting ready to once again embark on a world tour. And, I am single again. That is also my truth. Both stories, though contradictory, are concurrent with my reality. Talk about an out-there statement! Life is filled with circumstances that, in an instant, can affect everything we do from that moment on. Like my music, the impact of these circumstances is open to interpretation. That interpretation, like the truth, is subjective.

"Come to My Window," my biggest hit ever, has always been perceived as a love song, but it is really a song about being frustrated. On numerous occasions, I have written a song that started out as a love song but, by the time I recorded it, it had become a song about angst and desire and wanting and needing. And sometimes, people have thought of a song in a totally different way than I had intended it. Maybe that's what makes a good song good. It's certainly what gives it so much power. People use music to fit the circumstances of their own lives.

I am a songwriter. My job is to focus and balance the words and the music that live inside me and have lived there for most of

© 1995 Melissa Etheridge/Photo by Jodi Wille

Performing "Silent Legacy"   © 1996 MELISSA ETHERIDGE/PHOTO BY NICOLE BENGIVENO/MATRIX

my life. What you choose to do with them is up to you. Make my music the soundtrack to your life. Make it whatever you wish. Sometimes, through my songs, I get to share the pain of a breakup, and sometimes I am part of the seduction. Change the circumstances and there are days when I can understand, better than most, the obsessive feelings love can bring on, and I can feel that emptiness called loneliness. I look at it like this. If my music has the power to move and touch people, then ultimately that's what I am supposed be doing: writing music. I do not write songs to keep for myself. I give the songs away. And they become whatever the people listening want them to be. Just because a song came from this certain place—maybe anger, maybe passion, whatever—once I let it go, it takes on a life of its own. That's the beauty of creating music. It is something different to everyone. Someone once told me that a great piece of art is one that provokes an emotional response, whether positive or negative. I think the same can be said for music. You don't have to like it to feel something.

You see, I believe that people have their own points of view. This is simply mine.

The Truth Is...

Lonely Is a Child

...

IN THE MID-EIGHTIES, AS A LARK, I HAD A PAST-LIFE RE-gression. I WAS trying to find out why I'm a musician. Music didn't run in my family, and I don't believe that musical talent or ability is inherited anyway, so I just wanted to know if I was Mozart reincarnated, or something fun like that, in a past life.

So one day, my doorbell rings and in walks the classic Crone, a big old wise woman who sat me down on my floor and began talking to me, gently and quietly. It was hypnotic. The rhythm of her voice took me back to five years ago, ten years ago, fifteen years ago, and then ages three, two, one. I'm back in the womb, looking for a light to be born into. I follow the light and start talk-ing about being a half-Indian man in the 1800s. A doctor who died of scleroderma, a disease that hardens the skin. Then I go back far-ther and I'm an actor in a German cabaret in the 1600s. I was a woman dressed as a man, performing for a group of townspeople.

Who knows where all this stuff was coming from? It was bizarre. But very entertaining, very amusing, clearly all in fun. I just went with it. Then the woman began to bring me back, step by step, pulling me out of the regression, part of which is to guide you back into your current life through reexperiencing your own birth. She starts talking me through, saying, "You're in the birth canal." And I was feeling it. I could feel what it was like to be in the womb and then in the birth canal. And then, all of a sudden, I couldn't breathe. Out of nowhere, I was feeling this great pain in my legs. I started screaming and hollering and breathing really hard. The therapist was startled by my reaction, and she brought me out as quickly as she could for fear that I was really in pain. She said, "Whoa, okay. Okay, now you're being born—one, two, three, four— five—six—seven, eight, nine, ten! Okay, you're born. Whew!"

She asked me if my birth had been difficult. Not that I knew of. I had never heard anything about it. I called my mom as soon as I got home, and I explained to her that I had done this past-life regression and I wanted to know if there were any problems when I was born. "Well," she replied. "You were held back." Held back? What did that mean? My mom sort of fumbled through her words, and then, for the first time in twenty-five years, she told me the truth about my birth.

I was born in Leavenworth, Kansas, at Cushing Memorial Hospital, on May 29, 1961. My mother went into labor at home. As soon as she arrived at the hospital, they sedated her. That was the protocol in those days. It was one o'clock in the afternoon and all the doctors had just gone to lunch. My mother was ready to push and I was ready to be born, ready to enter the world and start my life. But it couldn't happen without a doctor being there. Of course, this was before there were pagers or cell phones, so the nurses held my mother's legs together so that I could not come out until someone could get the doctor. They held her legs together for fifteen minutes. Fifteen desperate minutes of struggling and straining to get out. Her uterine wall was pushing up against me and, as hard as I tried, I was not allowed to enter the world as planned. And so my first experience in this world was that I was being crushed. I was in terrible pain.

Mom isn't the kind of woman who would make a scene. Not even if she were giving birth. Mother never wanted to make trouble, especially on an emotional or spiritual level, even though everything in her body was telling her to let me out! She acquiesced, and said, "Okay, we'll wait for the doctor." That's right. She put the power in somebody else's hands, and all the while, I'm dying.

I was born severely black-and-blue and bruised. I had a hematoma, which became a birthmark on my chest that was there until I was twenty. And my mother had never said a word to me about it. For twenty-five years. That's my family: "We just won't talk about it." "Everything is fine." I survived, so we never talked about it. Ever. And we would probably have never talked about my birth experience if I hadn't had that past-life regression. I was born black-and-blue and close to death. I guess you can say that I was bruised from birth—figuratively and literally.

I was born on my older sister Jennifer's birthday. I don't think I was the present she was expecting that day she turned four. From my very first breath of life, I would be this "thing" that took attention away from her. Neither of us ever had our own birthday. We had to share the day like twins, without the joy of having a twin or the connection that comes from a twin relationship.

As far back as I can remember, my sister has been one of the most powerful influences on my life. Not in a good way, necessarily. But powerful. She was prettier, she was thinner, she was more tan, her hair was nicer. She took care of herself, she knew what clothes to wear. She had that whole girl thing I never really had.

I was very much a tomboy, completely awkward in my body. I wanted to be like her. My mother never showed me how to do my hair, how to dress "right." I still don't know how to braid hair, I never learned to wear makeup and I never dressed especially feminine. I didn't know how to do any of that girly stuff you're supposed to learn as a kid. I longed for that and, on many levels, in a strange way, I got that from my sister. But, what I also got from my sister has affected my ability to connect emotionally in every way.

One of my earliest memories of Jennifer is at around age three or four. We were playing in the basement of our house. She was trying to get me to drink a Coke. I did not like anything carbonated, and for the most part, I still don't. I can tolerate champagne, but just barely. I kept refusing to drink the Coke. I just didn't want to drink it. My sister finally decided to hold me down on the floor and forced the Coke down my throat. She just poured it into my mouth, choking me.

After all, she was angry at me from birth. I can only imagine that she was home, expecting to celebrate her fourth birthday, and her mother and father were nowhere to be found. She sat there alone—no party, no cake, no celebration—all because I was about to come into the world.

My family, who hid any sign of emotion, never explained to Jennifer that I wasn't a threat. All she knew was that whatever little love and attention she usually got on her birthday wasn't going to happen that day, and she has stayed angry and envious ever since. I felt cared for in my family, but I never felt safe. As a baby, I never learned to crawl. I scooted. There are home movies of me scooting, but none of me crawling. Experts say that this is a sign of fear. I also used to stick my finger in my ear, and my parents were concerned that maybe there was something wrong, but there wasn't. I guess it was just a comfort thing. Comfort and safety were two things I never really sensed when I was growing up. I think this lack of warmth and affection is the spine of a lot of issues that I still carry with me today.

Outside the home, of course, was a different story. Classic America. We lived about two miles from downtown Leavenworth, down a barely paved road packed with houses full of children. There were open fields and always something to do. Kickball. Baseball. So it looked perfectly normal. Except for the prisons. The Federal Penitentiary. The Kansas State Penitentiary for Men. The Kansas State Penitentiary for Women. And the Army Penitentiary. All of which were the main industry for the town. My best friend's dad was a guard at the prison. He used to walk to work. So it never seemed like anything out of the ordinary. Not at the time. The Federal Penitentiary had a dome, so it always looked like the Capitol Building as far as I was concerned. And I thought that every town had one.

As I got older, Jennifer got angrier and more physical. She used to torment me by hiding in the closet, or under my bed, and there was always this awkward silence just before she would jump out and scare me half to death. I knew she was hiding there and I'd just stand in the middle of the room and wait. Wait for her to scare me. To this day, I still can get frightened if someone hides and tries to scare me, even if it's just in fun. It was very manipulative and controlling behavior—two traits that today I find so attractive in other women, especially women I am romantically involved with.

When I was around six years old, things started to change with Jennifer. She began to want things from me. Things I was uncomfortable with. I know that all kids experiment and play doctor and that might have been all Jennifer thought it was, but it sure wasn't that to me. At night, in the bedroom of our home, she would be gentle with me, talking sweetly to me, which was curious in itself. She would tell me what to do and I would follow her directions. I would do as she asked. I knew that touching her was wrong and I knew that it was something that would never be talked about. Not in our family. I felt tremendous shame, though I didn't know what to call it at the time.

My mother's family was from Arkansas, right on the border of Louisiana and Texas. Just Southern, Southern, Southern. We'd go down and visit my grandparents in their house in El Dorado (that's El Dor-AY-do, not El Dor-ah-do). My grandfather was in the oil business and the whole place smelled like oil. The whole town. We'd visit for a bit. And then we'd all pile into the pickup, four grown-ups on the front seat, all the kids in the open back, and just drive down the freeway, eighty miles an hour. I'm surprised we didn't lose one of us, going so fast. We'd head over to my grandparents' cabin in Strong, Arkansas, which was in the middle of nowhere. We'd spend most of the summer there. Fishing in the pond. Playing. Just being out in the dirt.

In El Dorado, my sister and I would spend time alone. In the bedroom we shared. Or the playhouse outside. The same pattern repeated again. Where Jennifer would talk to me. Sweetly. Gently. Her pants would slide off and I would follow her directions. Her instructions: Do this, do that. The words sounded nice, but there's nothing nice about it. She wasn't my friend. It felt like something was being taken from me. And I felt horrible. Just horrible. I would step outside myself and just watch. I'd become an observer. Passing through.

And then, after it was over, I'd eat. My Grandma's white coconut cake. I'd sit at the kitchen table and fill myself up. Fill myself up with something that felt good. Tasted good. I'd give myself pleasure in the only way I knew how. Food. It never occurred to me to talk to anyone about this—about my sister or the way I felt. We didn't do that in my family. We didn't talk about things. Not ever.

My relationship with my sister went on this way for years. And it only stopped when I got up the courage to stop it. We were all of us going down to Arkansas one year, and before we got to our grandparents' house, we stopped at a hotel in Eureka Springs. My sister and I were standing in the bathroom, brushing our teeth, and she hit me right across the face, really *really* hard. It was like *pow!* It didn't make any sense at all. It was clear out of the blue. The television was on in the room. Bella Abzug was speaking at the 1972 Democratic National Convention. I was eleven years old. I just remember thinking to myself that this was all wrong. And that's when it stopped. That's when I said, enough. You have had enough of me. I stopped it. I removed myself from ever being in that situation with her again. I didn't spend time with my sister alone. Not unless I absolutely had to.

But I still felt empty. I felt like there was this hole inside me that needed to be filled. So I looked for ways to fill it up. Food was one. Movies were another.

I'd watch a film and dream that life could be like that: a world where everything's all nice and neat and people love each other, and then they're sad and they're angry and they're happy, and then it either turns out okay or everybody dies. There's always an ending in the movies, whether it is happy or sad. I thought, "That's the way life is supposed to be." I really believed in the fantasy of happily ever after and believed that you can find love that lasts forever. I believed in that Hollywood thing. Growing up, I had no other input on relationships, love, or life. Movies and television told me what it all should be and should mean. It was also a way that I could experience emotion. For two hours, sitting in a dark theater where no one else could see me—see me laugh, cry, or react to whatever was happening on the screen—I could escape the reality of my life and safely dream about my future. For those couple of hours, no one was going to say, "Don't do that," or "We don't react that way."

The one thing that did keep me safe, that gave me a feeling of comfort growing up, was music. Music took me somewhere safe—a place where I was happy and free and comfortable being myself. I knew from a very young age that music was something I wanted to be a part of. It was something that made me feel good and helped me escape to a place where life was how I always dreamed it should be. Where life was like the movies. Fairy-tale endings and unconditional love.

I remember hearing the Beatles for the very first time, in 1964. I was standing in my driveway and putting my ear to our tiny transistor radio. Even with the crackling, barely audible sound that the transistor radio made, I heard "I Want to Hold Your Hand" for the first time, and I thought that I had heard the voice of God. It was the most incredible thing I'd ever heard, and it moved me in a way I had never before experienced. I became obsessed with music.

After that, I had the radio on constantly. Johnny Dohlens, WHB, Kansas City. They played everything on the radio back then. Rock. Pop. Everything. And I'd listen to it all. No judgment. I'd listen to my parents' albums. They had everything from Neil Diamond to the Mamas and the Papas. Bolero to Janis Joplin and Crosby, Stills, Nash, and Young. My sister had much cooler albums like Humble Pie, Led Zeppelin, and George Harrison. Music was complete pleasure. Just like my Grandma's white coconut cake. I'd get completely absorbed into it, focused. I'm just completely there and the world goes away.

I'd listen to the music and I'd watch it, too. *The Ed Sullivan Show, The Dick Cavett Show, The Red Skelton Show.* I'd watch all the shows that had live music on them. And I'd watch the people singing the music. Making the music. Mick Jagger. The Beatles. But it was the Archies who were the most influential. I'd watch the Archies and then I'd get the neighborhood kids together, get all the pots and pans out, and do a show in the garage. I never wanted to be Betty or Veronica. I wanted to be Reggie. I always wanted to be Rock and Roll. I drew a big sign that said ARCHIES with a circle around it, put everyone in their place, and then we'd do a show. I was the lead guitarist of course. Jumping up and down with my badminton racquet. We'd play "Sugar, Sugar," Tommy James and the Shondells and Steppenwolf. Every day after school became "Magic Carpet Ride" time.

One day, my father came home with a real guitar for me. I hadn't even been asking for one. He just brought it home. I didn't know that he knew I was playing the badminton racquet. It was a Stella, by Harmony, which is actually a pretty good first guitar for a kid in Kansas. He bought it at Tarbot's Tune Shop in town. I would go down there late in the afternoons after school, and I would see my guitar teacher, Mr. Don Raymond, an old big-band jazz guitarist. I'm sure he had been a fabulous musician in his day, but a tragic accident cut off the fingers on his left hand, right at the knuckles. So he learned to play with his right hand. I was eight years old and it was pretty scary to look at his fingers, or what used to be his fingers, but he was a serious musician and he taught me to be a serious musician and to take my lessons very earnestly. I learned all of the notes on the guitar, one by one, string by string, every day, until I actually learned a song. It was a simple song, but it was the first song I ever learned and pretty soon those notes turned into chords and my chords turned into more songs. Before I knew it, I was playing "I Want to Hold Your Hand" and "Sugar, Sugar." Playing them for real. I was making the music. Not pretending anymore.

My mother's parents, Earl and Annie Lou Williamson

My sister and me, sharing another happy birthday

One of the only photos I have of my whole family together, Christmas 1998

After a horse show (left to right): me; my nephew, Joshua; Mom;
my niece, Jessica; and my sister, Jennifer

My sister and me,
at her high school
graduation, with Dad

I realized that once I had learned three basic chords, I could play just about anything. This opened up a whole new world to me—a world where I could perform and create. A world that was mine, that would accept me for who I was. Give me what I wanted. I became inspired and I found some peace in the process. Words began to flow from me and, at age ten, I wrote my first song using three silly little chords: "Don't Let It Fly Away." I rhymed words like *love* with *above*. I rhymed *bus* with *Gus*.

I found solace in my music that I didn't have before I learned to play. I would go into our basement and play my guitar to fill up my loneliness. My mother wouldn't really talk to me, and she wasn't too keen on my playing the guitar. But I played every day. And I would play when we traveled to Arkansas to visit my grandparents. I dearly loved my grandmother. She had that whole maternal nurturing thing that my mother didn't. She'd open all the drawers in the kitchen, pull out all the tools and the whisks and things. And she'd say, "Just go. Play." She would listen to me play the guitar, those same three chords over and over, and she was actually listening. She'd sit in her living room and listen to me sing and play song after song after song. After a few more trips, Grandma would still listen to me, but from then on, she was lying down in her bed. Unbeknownst to me, she was terribly ill. She had been stricken with cancer of the ovaries and breasts, and eventually her body was so riddled with it, the cancer metastasized everywhere. But she would listen joyfully all the same, lying there in her bed, and I played happily for her. When she would simply tell me that "Grandmother's not feeling well," I knew that it was time to let her get her rest.

My final visit with Grandmother was in the hospital, before she died. My visit needed special arrangements because children under the age of twelve were not allowed in the hospital. But I was this woman's granddaughter and I had showed up, with my guitar, to see my grandmother. I wanted to play my music for her, sing for her—comfort her. The nurses made an exception for me, and I was able to go into her room and sit beside my grandmother on her bed. I sang a new song I had just written—well, more like plagiarized—from a children's book. It was called "The Good Little Sheep." I sang to her with all of the tubes running in and out of her body—and with my grandmother in a state of semiconsciousness.

THE GOOD LITTLE SHEEP

The good little sheep run quickly and soft.
Their colors are gray and white.
They follow their leader nose to tail,
For they must be home by night.

I am sure that there were other verses to it—something about wanting to be a good little sheep. For all of her pain, my grandmother still listened. She listened to *me*. And when I was done, she turned to me and said, "When I die, will you put that song in my casket and bury it with me?" I kind of understood what was happening and what was going to happen. I felt a connection with my grandmother that was unique for me at that time in my life. She loved me unconditionally, and she was the only person I felt protected by as a child.

Of course, I couldn't express any of these emotions. I didn't know how. But I remember the feeling when she asked that question, that moment of physical realization that tingles through you when you know something important is happening. But there's no outlet for it. It's a life-and-death moment and I had no idea how to handle it. None of us did. So we don't handle it. We bury it. And move on.

So I looked at my grandmother and said, "Okay." I packed up my guitar and we went home, back to Leavenworth. One night, not too long afterward, I suddenly woke up in the middle of the night and became extremely ill. I stayed home from school that next day, and my mom came home and told me that my grandmother had passed away in the middle of the night. When my grandmother died, it was like everything just went *clunk!* I was in the sixth grade. I had given up being frightened of my sister and all of my raw, unharnessed emotion would, forever forward, be placed into my song writing. All I could think about on our way back to Arkansas for her funeral was her request to be buried with the lyrics to my song. I didn't want to go view her casket. I couldn't face seeing her lifeless body. So I wrote the lyrics down on a piece of paper and gave them to my aunt, who assured me that she would place them in the casket for me. At the funeral and in the limousine, all I could envision in my mind was that piece of paper and those words in her casket with her for all of eternity. I don't remember if I cried. I can't recall seeing my mother cry. We didn't do much crying in my family. That would have been a show of emotion, something we never did.

After the funeral, I wrote what I consider to be my first real song. It came from somewhere in my heart, somewhere in my soul, somewhere that had just been opened up inside of me. It was about a war orphan—something I didn't think that I knew anything about, but the truth is, I knew all too well the feeling of being an orphan. I have felt alone and abandoned during my whole life. The song was called, "Lonely Is a Child."

LONELY IS A CHILD

Trees are swaying in the wind
Things are so free
But I sit here waiting
For her to come home to me.

Lonely is a child waiting for his mother to come home,
Lonely is a child waiting for his mother, but a mother has he none . . .

When the war came to this land
Many years ago
She disappeared from my sight
And I just want to know
Where is she

A lot of my earliest songs were sort of sad and lonely. I would write about either the kind of love I never knew, or how I was pining for something or someone who had left me. Even as a teenager. Oh, and there were the typical teenager suicide songs. I was obsessed with dying and writing songs about dying. I went through a phase, around the eighth grade, of telling people that I was terminally ill. It got me attention and sympathy, which was exactly what I was looking for. I would have taken any show of emotion from another person. It's strange to look back. I was never personally thinking of suicide, but I was surely looking to be noticed as a teenager. I can still feel an incredible sadness, a need for emotion, and a sensation of being in my adolescent pain. Things were so bleak in my head that I even went so far as to call a troubled-teen hotline and attend a group therapy class to talk about my dark feelings. I met a girl there whose soul was even angrier and more abused and tortured than mine. She just sat in the corner and didn't talk to anybody. I went home and wrote a song about her. I completely understood that type of darkness and agony. It's an adolescent feeling that can bring on the idea of suicide. I am too ego-driven to have ever gone through with suicide—that's for sure. I guess I just wanted someone to notice me and it came out in the lyrics to the songs I wrote as a teen. One song is called "Stephanie."

STEPHANIE

Stephanie, oh Stephanie,
What pain do you see?
What's in your eyes?
You sit down, you have a smoke
But never a word have you spoke.
Stephanie, all the lines are dead—
I wish I knew what's goin' on in your head.
Reach out, oh reach out to me.
Oh Stephanie, can't you see—
If you ever need, I am here.
Stephanie, what lingers in the hallway
In the dark corners of your mind?
And the writing that is on the wall—does it say it all?
What will I find?
What key unlocks your door?
What do you tell yourself when
You're crying for more?
But maybe someday when your soul's set free
And the sun beams through, maybe then I may see.
Stephanie, pick up the broken pieces of glass
On your windowsill to the world.
I know inside the dark stormy shell
There's a bright shining beautiful pearl.

I kept playing my guitar and I started to sing for my friends. We would sing and play together. Linda Stuckey and Chris Luevane, who were in my class in school, learned to sing "Lonely Is a Child," and we began to perform as a group. We were so sincere, so sad, and *so* in the sixth grade. Chris called me up one day all excited about an upcoming talent show at the Leavenworth Plaza. She was certain that we ought to sing in it and so we did. We got up on stage and sang from the deepest part of our sixth-grade hearts. It was incredible. It seemed like thousands of people were watching. There were really about fifty. All the friends and relatives of the people in the talent show, probably. The MC was a man named Bob Hammill. He was a ventriloquist with this Charlie McCarthy sort of doll. He'd do a bit and then introduce the next act. The Shortz Sisters, who sang country music all done up in their spangly country-western gear. The Shroyer Sisters in their little pink outfits, doing their acrobatic act. Very exotic. Back bends and splits and the whole thing.

And then it was our turn. Chris and Linda and I walked out on stage. And I stared out at the audience. It was my first time in front of an audience. My heart was beating so fast. I'm dizzy and I can barely breathe. And then I hit the first note and I play. And Chris and Linda just disappear. There's just me and the audience. And the music. When I finished, there was applause. I walked off stage and it was the most connected I'd ever felt in my entire life. Connected to heart. Connected to want. Connected to experience. It was like a drug. A drug that made me *alive*.

Little Tommy Williams won the talent contest with his rendition of "Okie from Muskogee." But we were finalists and were given a trophy. A very small trophy. Years later, I was presented again with that trophy while visiting Leavenworth for my tenth high school reunion. The trophy is in the photograph on the back of the *Breakdown* album. I keep it in my display case at home, right next to my Grammy Awards.

Soon after the talent contest, Bob Hammill called and told us he was putting together a variety show with some of the other acts from the contest, the Shortz Sisters and the Shroyer Sisters, something he could take around town, perform at old folks' homes, the V.A. center, all the prisons. Prisons have the most enthusiastic audiences: 2,000 people who want to be entertained. You might say they're the ultimate captive audience. Once, we were stuck inside a prison for an hour because there was a stabbing or something, and all the prisoners were locked down. But as soon as it got cleared up, off we went, into the auditorium. It was hilarious, really; these little girls performing for criminals. The Shroyer Sisters in their little leotards doing splits and backbends always got a very enthusiastic response from the inmates.

We played the Kansas State women's prison and I remember standing on stage, staring out at the inmates, and thinking, "What are all these men doing inside a women's prison?" It took a while for me to realize that they *were* women. And once I had that realization, I was curious about them, interested. Not on a conscious level, of course, but there was something going on in that prison that fascinated me.

The Bob Hammill Variety Show was great fun for all of us. It's where I learned how to get up in front of people and perform. No matter where the stage was—local schools, old folks' homes, wherever—I loved it. I loved the attention. I loved the warmth. I loved the appreciation. I loved the spotlight. I felt secure and loved and safe and at home on stage.

The stage became the safest, most rewarding place that I have ever been. I am allowed to open up everything about myself on stage. Being on stage worked so well for me emotionally that, for the longest time, it was all I wanted to do. I would have done anything to do it on as large a scale as I possibly could. Like the

*Performing in the
Bob Hammill
Variety Show*

Me, at age four

I was ten years old when
I wrote my first song,
"Don't Let It Fly Away."

Think of all the chil[dren]
[Al]throughout the la[nd]
Think of everybody
a holding hands
why don't you come a[nd]
join the dream wit[h]
Don't let it fly away
Don't let it fly away
Don't let it fly away it's love!
Everybody's gonna
~~be~~ one man
And when I get older
I'm gonna take a stand
You'll see me then
with my brothers hand oh!
Don't let it fly away
Don't let it fly away
Then ole gods gonna come down it's LOVE!
and see all os us
he's gonna see me and you
~~yes not he'll even see old guys~~
Then he's gonna [s]hake hands
yos on all of us
Don't let it fly away
Don't let it fly away
Don't let it fly away it's LOVE!
Song called (It's Love)

movies, it was an escape for me. Performing gave me the ability to hide out and be who I wanted to be, and be loved and feel safe and secure.

As I became more serious about my music, I would ask my parents for their opinion from time to time about my career choice: to be a rock-and-roll star. These conversations were kind of funny, coming from an eleven-year-old girl. Dad was supportive, but he never planned on my dreams ever coming true for me. He'd say fatherly things like, "Well, I believe that only one in a million persons can ever become successful at it, and we want you to know that the chances of disappointment are probable and huge, but we don't want to discourage you from something that you love." Somehow, I think my parents believed that my interest in music was a passing phase, and if it did persist, I could always become a music teacher. They never discouraged me, but they never gave a lot of credence to what I was doing.

My optimism—my naïve teenage buoyancy telling me that I could make it—came from inside of me. It wasn't a developed hopefulness from my surroundings. It was all my doing. My ambition drove my success. Even as a child. From my very first gig, I saved all the money I made. Dad bought me my first guitar, but from that point forward I bought everything else from my own money—every sound system, every amp, and every instrument I played.

Dad would drive me to band practice or to a gig. He never said no to me about that. There were venues that wouldn't allow me in because of my age, unless one of my parents was there. And Dad was always happy to oblige. I was twelve years old when I started playing in adult groups like the Wranglers. We played lots of country and western, and we performed in local bars around Leavenworth. Until I was a senior in high school, I played with a bunch of different bands—the Showmen, the Mid-West Express, the Road Show. I learned at an early age how to duck away from a flying beer bottle and how not to get hit in the face with a microphone if a drunk patron accidentally fell onto the stage.

I was myopic in my thinking. I could see only one thing: my future as a singer/songwriter. But first, I had to "learn the trade." There are some people who would say that, as a child, I wasn't necessarily as gifted a singer as I thought I was. They found my voice too raspy and harsh. At one point, even my mother said that I wasn't born with a great voice but I taught myself to have one. In an effort to help me, my parents sent me to a singing coach who had been a classically trained vocalist. She had sung at the Metropolitan Opera. She was a great vocal teacher. I was just not a malleable student. I tried to sing these Italian arias, but she understood that I sang from my soul, in a raw, untrained way. Clearly, this was going nowhere. She said, "As long as you just breathe right. . . ." I would listen and breathe from my diaphragm, and I became aware of how to pronounce words while singing. That was all she could give me. After three lessons, she told me: "I want you to go home and I want you to tell your parents not to waste their money because you're going to sing the way you sing and I shouldn't try to teach you how to sing differently."

As my confidence on stage grew, I finally thought I had reached level ground. A safe place where I could be who I was, who I wanted to be outside of my family. Life's never that easy, is it? By the time I got to eighth grade, things started to get very confusing for me.

Ready to Love

...

PEOPLE ALWAYS ASK ME: WHEN DID I KNOW I WAS GAY? The answer I've always given is: "I had a crush on my kindergarten teacher." Which I did. But the truth, as always, is a little more complicated than that.

My first kiss was in the sixth grade, with Mike Strange. I suppose we were doing what most kids at that age do, running around and chasing each other. We were in a dark basement, listening to the Temptations singing "Just My Imagination," when we kissed for the first time. It was one of those closed-mouth kisses, awkward and passionless. We were twelve years old and the world was still filled with tremendous possibilities. We danced and listened to music. We would see each other in school and talk on the phone. He was my boyfriend.

When adolescence started to set in, so did my confused feelings. I guess my adolescence wasn't really any different than anyone else's. It's when you discover your sexuality—the point where you experiment and become who you're going to be. I realized that while most of my friends were all excited about whether this guy or that guy was going to ask them out or to the football game, I was wondering why my best friends would rather be going with them instead of me. All of a sudden, the girls that I liked as my best friends, I REALLY liked, if you know what I mean. I started to question what it was that I really wanted from these friendships, which were becoming ever more important in my life. Too important. My friends couldn't just be my friends, they had to be devoted to me. I had to have their focus all the time. They had to *love* my music. I was filling myself up with them—with their attention, their concerns. Of course I wasn't dealing with what was really going on. I didn't *know* what was really going on.

I went to a Christian youth summer camp when I was a teenager, and there was one particular girl I became rather fixated on. Her name was Jo, and, man, did I have a crush on her. I didn't understand my obsessive feelings toward her at the time, but they certainly complicated things for me. I couldn't quite figure out that what I was feeling was sexual and not just emotional. It was never a question of wanting to kiss her, or being attracted to her. It was about so much more. More than she could have ever given me. More than I would ever get. I wanted to be with her every minute of every day. When I was with her, I felt great. When I wasn't, I felt desperate—alone and confused. But the more I wanted from her, the clearer it became that I was going to get nothing, so I just cut it off—completely. She, of course, never understood my emotional hot-and-cold behavior. I recently found my diary from 1975 and the entries are just hilarious to me. On one side of the page I am professing my love for a boy named Melvin. Missy-'n'-Melvin, TLA. And directly next to that page is my frustration over why I can't see Jo, and wanting to tell her how I felt, but being so scared and uncertain of how she would react. She tried to make plans with me, but I just wasn't capable of having her in my life. My feelings were too strong and I had no clue how to handle the situation. I have always felt so sorry about doing that to her because of my own lack of understanding of what was going on inside of me. But, the truth is, I had a big crush on this girl, and it completely freaked me out!

I had nowhere to put these feelings, no one to talk to about them. I didn't know where to turn, didn't even know how to talk about it, much less anyone to talk to about it . . . And then one day, in ninth grade, my social studies teacher kept me after school. She was this really sweet, caring, special lady. She sat me down in the empty classroom and she told me a story about a girl she had gone to college with. I listened carefully, not quite sure of what she was saying to me. She told me that she had had a friend in college who she really loved a lot. They spent all of their time together. One day, this girl called my teacher and played the Beatles' "And I Love Her" over the phone for her. I couldn't believe what my teacher was telling me. It made a huge impact on me because I was feeling all sorts of things in school, so unsure of what it all meant. I was feeling insane, but my teacher—who, incidentally, was married—was letting me know in her own way that there were people like me out there in the world. She reassured me that I was not crazy. I didn't know what she was trying to say at the time, but, a couple of years later, it all made sense and I am so grateful for her gesture. That kind of tolerance and support was hard to come by in Leavenworth when I was growing up.

But there was still the sense that these feelings, these romantic feelings I was having for other girls, were something I just should not talk about. So I didn't. I tried to fit in just like everybody else. So, like everyone else, I dated boys in high school.

I had a boyfriend at the end of my sophomore year. It was mostly a summer fling. He had just graduated and was getting ready to go to college in the fall. We had a lot in common. He was a musician—a saxophone player and a really, really good one. We sort of had a band together, playing big-band numbers. His buddies were horn players, and I remember writing a song with him and it was a lot of fun to do that with someone I liked. I remember telling him my dream of becoming a famous rock star, and his response was, "Well, that's all fine and good but when I get married I want my wife to stay home." That was a big lightbulb over my head, and I realized that, no, that would not be okay with me. I was never going to be someone's stay-at-home wife. I wasn't going to let anyone get in the way of my dream. That idea, that dream, was so much more important to me than any person could ever be in my life. That much I was sure of.

We were boyfriend and girlfriend all summer long, and he was my first real sexual experience. We never actually had sex, but we did just about everything else. I remember it as just being very clinical in my head. I remember thinking, "I wonder what I'm missing here." I wanted to know what sex was all about because all my friends were so into it and I just wasn't getting the same feelings they were getting. I didn't feel anything, but I didn't know exactly what I was supposed to be feeling anyway. I had nothing to compare it to. He was all hot and horny and everything, and I tried to get into it. One day he came to me and told me that he had been reading "Dear Abby" and the column was about women who are frigid. Frigid? Like a refrigerator? I just stared at him, not really sure what he meant. What am I supposed to be? I didn't realize that he was talking about my physical response to him. And of course I couldn't really take that in or relate how I was feeling about him to my feelings about girls. So I just shut him out. Like a door slamming.

*The Showmen
and me. I was
thirteen years old here.*

Our Road Show promotional photo

*An entry from my
diary in 1976*

Having no one to talk to about all these feelings sure made me a better songwriter. I'd disappear into my basement for hours at a time—singing, writing. I began to create whole worlds inside my lyrics. Worlds that made sense. Worlds where I could say whatever I wanted to.

In those days, I wrote about all sorts of things I had *never* seen or experienced firsthand. I had a vivid imagination and learned to use my imagery effectively in my lyrics. I wrote songs about how cold it was in New York in December, but I had never been to the Big Apple. To some degree, I was also writing about girls, though I was unaware of it at the time. I would change the lyrics from "you were" to "he was" so that I could veil my true feelings. I was always missing someone. I was tortured by my need for love and affection—my need to find someone who could fill up the emptiness inside me. I'm still driven by that need as a songwriter. The best songs I write are still the songs that have an I'm-so-very-sad-and-alone theme.

For a few weeks, in the beginning of my junior year, all of this changed. There was a new boy in school. His parents had just moved to Leavenworth with the army. He was the classic good-looking American boy: blond, handsome, star of the football team. And he asked *me* to go to the homecoming dance. Me, a tomboy who didn't know how to do all those girly things. My friend Laura had a huge crush on this boy and she was shocked that he asked me, "I can't *believe* he asked *you*." It's not like I was an ugly duckling or anything. I just didn't know how to do pretty. Makeup wasn't even a concept in my life. And it was such a great surprise. I was completely excited about my date and the dance. For two weeks, I was thinking about my hair and my dress, and I was just normal. That fantasy Kansas dream. The football player. Homecoming. Normalcy.

We went to the dance—some streamers in the gym, records blaring from a bad PA system. I asked him if he wanted to dance. I have always loved getting out on the dance floor. I kept saying, "Let's dance." He kept turning me down, just flat out saying, "No, I can't." I thought he meant that he couldn't dance, as in he didn't know how to dance. But he explained to me that dancing was against his religion. His father was a preacher, and dancing was expressly forbidden. It was like a scene from the movie *Footloose*! I had never heard of such a thing. So I sat there at the homecoming dance with him, just sat there on the bleachers and talked to him for the rest of the night. He drove me home and walked me to my door, the perfect gentleman. Standing on my doorstep, I looked up at him. After all, this was the big-kiss-at-the-end-of-the-night moment, and I was a little nervous. But he just stuck out his palm to shake my hand. And I shook his hand good-night. But, as he turned to leave, I asked him, "Why did you ask me to the dance?" He told me that I was the safest person to ask because if he went to the dance with me, he wouldn't be tempted to sin. I just said good night, turned around, and thought to myself, "Thanks!" It was a huge adolescent "ouch."

But that's how relationships with boys were. Confusing. Full of mystery and a set of rules that I never seemed to understand. I went on a date with a boy named Hector once. He was a dark-skinned Cuban boy who had this crazy accent. Hector was cool as could be. The girls just *loved* him. We had a great time together, laughing, talking. And then I made a joke about being his girlfriend. Suddenly, Hector became totally serious. He looked at me and said: "You can't be my girlfriend. You're Missy Etheridge." He was staring at me, telling me I'm different. And I just didn't get it. It was all so confusing—the way that other people seemed to know things about me that I didn't. I started to think that nothing about dating or relationships would ever make any sense.

And then I met Jane. It's not her real name, but I'll call her that to protect her privacy.

Jane was very popular, with lustrous hair and beautiful fair skin. She was quiet and mysterious with a hidden sadness that I found so attractive. I *had* to make her my best friend. And I did. For a year, we had a friendship that became very obsessive. She was emotional—endlessly emotional. She cried at my songs. She was delightfully unhappy, and I loved it because she could show all of her emotions. I was completely, maniacally, in love with her. I know that every high school has two girls who are in this kind of friendship, but it was never a concept in my head that we were "the lezzies." In fact, I thought that was a term for someone who was weird or just didn't fit in. I never realized it was a reference to a girl who was gay.

Jane and I grew closer and closer. I had my music—I played all over the state on the weekends—and I had Jane. At the time, it seemed like enough. There were moments, though—moments that caused me to take a step back from the relationship and wonder about it. In my junior year, Jane and I went to a football game. I spent most of the night talking to another girl, who was a year older than me. Her name was Mary and she was beautiful, with dark skin, dark hair, and bewitching eyes. She was definitely my type. After the game, Jane and I walked to the parking lot and stood there for a minute. But then, out of nowhere, she turned around and slapped me. Just like Jennifer in the bathroom. Whack! She was so mad. She screamed at me for spending the whole night talking to Mary. Her jealousy was so scary. But it was also attractive. After all, if she got that angry, then she must really like me. I came from a family where there was never this type of reaction—no show of emotion, no passion. Jane's reaction was justified in my mind as caring. I soaked it up like a sponge that had never had this kind of passion before. So *this* is what it's like: passion, obsession, fervor, and infatuation. From my past, the only thing I had to compare this to was my relationship with my sister. She had hit me a couple of times, and Jennifer could turn on a dime, just like Jane: nice one minute and plain mean the next. That's all I knew about physical relationships with women. Jane was mirroring Jennifer's behavior, so I guess I thought that this is what love was supposed to feel like. It just fit.

Of course, you don't have to be Freud to see where this was going. Step by step, it was clear that choosing women, especially women who were going to be unavailable to me, was going to become a habit of mine—one that would be extremely hard to break. Let's face it, like Jo or Jane, part of the attraction was the forbidden nature of the whole thing. Attraction, for me, is very cerebral. It's a mental game. If I like you and you like me, then I would never go out with you. It's too easy, too predictable, too accessible. Ah, but if I like you and you reject me, like my mother or my sister did, then it is a familiar place for me. I'm trying to get from other people what they are simply not capable of giving to me. Wanting it. Needing it. Craving it. Obsessing over it. But never attaching the concept of ever receiving it.

I wasn't having conscious thoughts of wanting to kiss my best friend—not until it happened, anyway. Jane and I were having a sleepover at her house on my seventeenth birthday. We'd gone to see *Saturday Night Fever* at the drive-in. We laid in bed, and we held hands. And we touched. And when she rolled over, I leaned over her and I kissed her. It was this glorious kiss. It was everything I had ever felt, turned inside out. The sky opened up. It was fireworks. It was like an explosion went off inside my body, and suddenly, in that

That's funny, she doesn't look like a rock star . . .

Saying hello to old friends at my concert in Leavenworth, 1994

My senior prom date, Maurice Young

moment, I was a new person. I understood what it was I had been missing. I knew that this is who I was. This was my dream. I was going to leave Leavenworth and become famous, and I would have love in my life. I was ready to love . . . women.

READY TO LOVE

I look at you and all I can see is the shadow of my life.
You see this stage is a mirror. You can see me,
but I can't see past its light.
Others have tried to reach down inside.
I only said that they were wrong.
But when all I've got left is me and my pride
I realize you can't buy love with a song.

Somebody take me out of the night.
Show me what life is made of.
Won't somebody reach inside of my heart.
I think that I'm ready to love.

A lesson that's learned too late is a crime.
I can't stand the pain of what could have been.
It's such a shame, there's no one to blame.
Yet no one knows what I've seen.
What do you see when you look at me?
Do I really seem so far away?
But the song will go on and you will applaud.
And look at me, I'll just keep singing.

Somebody take me out of the night.
Show me what life is made of.
Won't somebody reach inside of my heart.
I think that I'm ready to love.
I think I'm ready to love.
I feel like I'm ready to love.

Senior year of high school was fast approaching, and I decided I wanted to change things—really spend my last year in school being a kid. So I stopped playing at bars. I let the band I had been working with know that I was going to spend this last year being just a normal kid. I devoted myself to school, to that whole social world, and to Jane, who I had started sleeping with on a regular basis. Jane and I spent so much of our time together, it bordered on the obsessive. We even worked together at a fast-food joint. Jane worked the counter and I was the packer. It was a totally boring job, but I was happy with it because Jane and I got to work together.

Until the day I walked in and realized that her name wasn't on the schedule for the next week. As I looked closer, neither was mine. I asked the manager what was going on and she got a little uncomfortable. "Well, I had to fire Jane because she wasn't doing a very good job. And, well, just figuring the way you two are, I had to let you go too." I stared at this woman, shocked. My relationship with Jane was such a private, secret thing, I had no idea that other people could see it, could feel it. And would react to it in such a strange way.

Jane wasn't making any plans for college, but my parents were pushing it all the time. College, college, college. If college was going to get me out of Leavenworth, then I was all for it. Of course the only thing I was going to study in college was music. And my choices were pretty limited. Juilliard, Oberlin, Eastman, all the other classical music schools where the only thing I could study was classical guitar, which I was definitely not interested in. The only place where it seemed like I could do what I wanted, where I could focus on being the singer–songwriter I always saw myself as, was at Berklee College of Music, in Boston. I applied and was accepted.

As the time to go got closer, my relationship with Jane got more tumultuous. After all, she wasn't going anywhere, just back to her job at another fast-food place. Right after I graduated from high school, I celebrated my eighteenth birthday. *Celebrating* might be too strong a word for it. It was miserable. Everyone seemed to forget about it. My father brought home a new sports car for himself, and most of the day seemed focused on that. My mother did give me a set of luggage for graduation, though. I never understood that. Maybe she knew I was ready to leave Leavenworth, or maybe she was telling me to go. Either way, I left shortly thereafter.

I Don't Think
We're in Kansas Anymore

...

MY PARENTS FLEW WITH ME TO BOSTON TO MOVE ME IN at Berklee. I must have brought ten pieces of luggage—everything I owned at the time. I'd never moved anywhere, so I had no idea how much I was supposed to bring. They got me all signed in and dropped me off in my dorm room at Berklee. It was right in the middle of town, on Massachusetts Avenue in Boston's Back Bay. My parents left and there I was. Alone in a new city. Ready to start my life away from home.

And in walked my roommate—Helene, from New York City. She was all fashion and style, with a huge presence. She was the first Jewish person I ever encountered in my life, and she was just so . . . different from anyone I was used to. Really out there, ready to make her mark on the world. That first night, we just sat up and talked. When I told her I was from Kansas, her eyes lit up. "Oh my God!" she said, like I was some slightly oddball foreigner. But eventually the conversation got more personal. Helene leaned into me and asked, "Well, do you like boys?"

What a funny question. No one ever asked me before if I liked boys. "Well, sure. They're fine. They're okay, I guess." Helene smiled at me and said "Because I don't. I like girls." And I sat straight up, thinking, "She's just like me! She likes girls!" It was such a revelation! There were other people like me. Other people I could talk to about my desires, in a free and open way. She told me that there were bars we could go to, and she intimated a whole world of women that I had no idea existed. In so many ways, my life started that day, during that conversation with Helene. After that, it was all different. She showed me a way to be, and I followed it.

A couple of weeks later, Helene walks up to me and says, "I found out where the women's bar is. It's called Prelude and it's right down the street." So off we go. And Helene waltzes right in, "Hey, sister," she says at the door. I show them Jennifer's expired ID to get in, and I walk inside. And it was just . . . wonderful. A room packed with women. Women of all shapes and sizes. Butch, tomboy, lipstick. Jewish women, women of color, white women— just this wonderful mix of people laughing and drinking and having a great time. What struck me most was women dancing together. Women, together, in public. I love to dance. In high school I'd go to the mixers, the dances, with Jane, and all I wanted to do was dance with her, lose myself in the music with her. But of course I couldn't. Not in Kansas, anyway.

It was shocking and wonderful all at the same time. It opened a door that I didn't even know existed. As I walked around the city, my whole perspective began to change. I realized that there was a whole gay world out there, a world that I'd never seen before and didn't even suspect existed. A world where I could be who I am. Where I could, at last, have a real sense of community. I started going to Prelude every weekend. I'd just sit at the bar, sip a drink, and watch.

It's not like school was a big pull on my time. I'm not quite sure what I expected at Berklee, but whatever it was, I didn't get it. All of the classes were very theory-driven, very caught up in the *idea* of music rather than the music itself. I had to learn to play a certain way. Learn all of their rules. I didn't like it. I thought that music was whatever it wanted to be. Theory just wasn't where I was at. I wanted to play. Not talk about it; *do* it.

Jane called me and told me she wanted to come visit. Sitting at the bar at Prelude was great, but it wasn't a relationship. Even then, I knew that was what I wanted. So I told Jane to fly on up. Her visit ended up with her moving into my dorm with Helene and me. I had to sneak her into the dorm time after time because, clearly, she wasn't a student there. Eventually, we decided to move into an apartment together. Which would mean, of course, that I had to get a job.

I worked security at Boston Deaconess Hospital. With my uniform and my time clock, I'd walk my rounds making sure everything was okay. It was a real job, something I'm not too fond of. I'd work the morning shift (from eight to five), and sometimes pull a double if they needed me to. And then I'd try and go to school. But the pull of school got less and less. After all, I had a job and I had Jane. But I hated that job, really hated it. I woke up one morning and said to myself, "I want to play music. I played music before and made money, I can do it again. I can." So I picked up my guitar and walked down into the Park Street subway station. I opened up my guitar case and just started playing all the songs I remembered from playing the bars and stuff. The people would all be standing there, waiting. When there weren't any trains, the sound down there was beautiful. My voice and the music reverberated through the whole station. People would drop money in, listen for a moment, and, just when I was in the middle of a song, the train would blast through, blaring, and all the people would just disappear. And I'd start singing all over again.

I did it that day and made something like eight dollars in the first hour. I counted it up and realized that it was more than Boston Deaconess was paying me. So I picked up one of my just-earned quarters, called the hospital from the station, and quit right there, on the spot. If I was going to have a job, it was going to be playing music. Music and nothing else.

I started at the top of Boylston Street and worked my way down, stopping in every bar and asking, "Do you have live music?" I got turned down flat at every single place until I got to a little downstairs restaurant and bar across from Hancock Center: Ken's By George. The manager told me to come back later for an audition. I came back and got a job playing five to nine (during cocktail hour). Five nights a week, fifty bucks cash a night. Two hundred and fifty bucks a week, off the books. I was living large.

I brought that first two hundred and fifty dollars home and showed it to Jane. She plucked it right out of my hand. Suddenly, she was deciding how to spend the money, what to do with it. I was sort of stunned. Why was she taking *my* money? But I didn't make a big deal of it. I couldn't. I would have been making a scene. And, of course, I didn't do that. I just let it slide off my back.

Playing at Ken's was great. It offered such freedom. Every night, I would go and just play for four hours. There was such a camaraderie there among the workers; we always had the best time. One woman, a customer, came back to see me a number of times. My age; well-dressed. And she started talking to me, chatting me up. She was clearly interested, and I wasn't about to let this opportunity pass me by. After work we drove around for a while. And then parked.

When I got home, Jane was upset. Very upset. A couple of days later, we were having breakfast and she just turned around and hit me. Boom! Right across the face. Gave me a black eye and a bloody nose. I was stunned, I didn't know what to do. "That was for the other night," she said. "I was just thinking about it and it made me so angry." That was the moment, I think, when I knew that I had to get out of that relationship. But I didn't act; I just went numb. I willed myself not to feel, thinking that it was the price I had to pay for stepping out on Jane. It was a repeat of my sister yelling at me or my mother hiding when I was young. I just turned it all off and pretended it wasn't even there.

Was my relationship with Jane love or addiction? In my head, that is an ongoing debate about many of my relationships. I eventually saw that Jane's jealousy was more of a sickness than a positive kind of emotion. It was no longer exciting to me; it became suffocating and difficult to take. It got to where I could talk to no one. She didn't want me to have any friends of my own. To this day, I don't know what her issues were from childhood. I never knew what circumstances from her own life taught her to snap like that. What I did know was that I had to get out from under her control. She had always hinted at suicide and said that she didn't think she would be able to go on if I ever left her. I had to get out of that relationship. I even opened up the Yellow Pages one day, to call a therapist for help. I explained to Jane that there was something wrong with me and that I needed to go and talk to someone so that I could figure out how to fix myself. In reality, I needed to go to someone who could help me figure out how to get out of this harmful and abusive relationship.

In the meantime, the door had been opened to other women, and I didn't want to close it. I started staying out more and more nights, longer and longer.

Finally, Jane decided she'd had enough. She told me she was going back to Kansas. I'm sure she wanted me to try and stop her, but I didn't. I was relieved. It was hard—trying to reconcile the woman I was becoming with the girl that I had been.

After Jane left, I felt like a weight had been lifted from my shoulders. I could come and go as I pleased, see whoever I wanted to, like Caroline. Caroline was a regular at Ken's, and the more she watched me play, the more I developed a crush on her.

Caroline came from a very wealthy family, and she was very smart. She was working as a sales associate at a high-end jewelry store. She was a lot of fun to hang around with, though she was a bit of a partier. I had developed a big crush on Caroline, and, as hard as I tried, I couldn't get next to her because she, of course, had a crush on someone else—one of the other girls in the group that night. I had a classic Melissa-type hopeless obsession. I like you, you like her, blah, blah, blah. We slept together one time, but we never had sex. Caroline was fun—sweet and warm. These were traits Jane hardly ever showed me. It was just nice to wake up with Caroline in the morning, and that's what inspired me to write the song "Morning," which has never been recorded. Why do musicians get their hearts broken? So they can write incredibly sad songs.

MORNING

Morning creeps into the window
Its golden fingers touch the sheets where we lay
Morning wraps its arms around me
And whispers in my ear it was all yesterday

Morning, you're lying here beside me
But somehow now the night feels so many years away
And it's morning, it's morning, it's morning

This moment, the end of all beginning
We just go on with living and be what we are
A memory lingers deep inside me
I must believe you loved me, if just for an hour
Longing to be the one you dream of
But someone else has touched that place in your heart
And it's morning, it's morning, it's morning

Love, love is so unfair
Its eyes are blind and its heart doesn't care
If it's left out in the rain
It's me that feels the pain

Morning there's no one left to save me
And all you ever gave me was the need to write a song
And it's morning, it's morning, it's morning

One night, I walked into Ken's for my regular gig and the
manager pulled me aside. And fired me. For no reason at all that I
can see, Ken's fired me right then and there. I was sorry about losing the job, sorry to leave a place that had become so familiar to me,
but I figured another job couldn't be too hard to find.

Little did I know. I got a job in a Japanese restaurant in Back
Bay. It closed two weeks after I started. Then another job at a
piano-bar-type place called 99's, but I didn't know enough show
tunes to make the gig stick. Finally, I landed a piano-bar job at the
Copley Hotel, a famous historic hotel right on Copley Plaza in
downtown Boston. Two days before I was supposed to start, the
hotel burned down. It was almost funny, but I couldn't help but feel
like someone was trying to tell me something.

Boston was good for me. It opened doors I didn't know existed. It changed me as a woman, as a lesbian, as a performer. But as I looked around this city, I realized that it wasn't where I wanted to be. I wanted to go west, to Los Angeles. After all, how else do you get to be a rock-and-roll star but by going to L.A.?

But I needed to make some money first, and the easiest place to do that was in Kansas. So I headed home.

Home Again

. . .

AFTER A YEAR IN BOSTON, I WAS ABLE TO LOOK AT LEAVenworth with new eyes. There were other gay people there. It was a revelation: a whole queer community that I never even knew had existed when I lived there. I started meeting new people and seeing old friends who, even if they weren't out of the closet, were open about who they are with their friends. The musical opportunities in Leavenworth, though, are less than stellar. I landed a job with the Army Chapel as its Music Assistant. I moved back in with my parents while I tried to scrape together enough money to buy a car so that I could drive to Los Angeles. I'd see Jane every so often, only through mutual friends. But it wasn't the same. The passion, the desperate need—it wasn't there anymore. Generally, I tried to steer clear of her. After the time we had spent together in Boston, she scared me. I had closed all the doors that would allow me to feel anything about her, and I wasn't about to open them again.

One of my friends was still a senior at Leavenworth High. I was twenty. She was eighteen. Before the end of the school year, I used to drop her off in the mornings and we'd listen to the radio in my car before class. She kept hinting that she knew that I was gay and she was very interested in me. She came on to me in a certain way—a very innocent way. Looking back on it, I now understand that she was looking to experiment and explore her sexuality.

I had never met her parents, but I knew that they were really strict. After school was over, we saw each other a couple of times and just kissed, which was kind of interesting. One day, she disappeared and I didn't know what had happened to her. A few weeks later, she came back home. I saw her one time and she explained to me that her parents had sent her away to a hospital to cure her of this "problem." I guess they'd found out that she was seeing me. I don't really know what happened. But there was resentment in her words when she told me what had happened. I felt like I had brought this on her. It was so overwhelming to me at the time. Because I was so into my world and myself, what was going on between us was perfectly okay with me. My mother, in her own way, was making it clear to me that she didn't approve of my lifestyle, but my parents would never have sent me away for being a homosexual. It kind of stunned me, the way that people would treat their children as if they were broken, and I sort of put it in the back of my head and tried to ignore it.

My mother had subtly let me know that she didn't approve of my lifestyle, but she had never verbally expressed it to me. Then I brought home Lisa, a girl I was seeing, and she spent the night with me. When I woke up, there was this note on the kitchen counter from my mother: "I don't know the nature of your psychological illness, but do not bring that girl over here anymore. If you're going to continue this behavior, you can't live in this house." That letter just cut me like a knife. Of course, my mother and I never spoke of the letter afterward. There was no further communication on the subject between the two of us.

But it did cause me to question myself. I knew that I was having these "unnatural" feelings. I never figured that my mother knew. And I was crushed by her response. Surprisingly, my mother's letter prompted me to seek guidance about my feelings of homosexuality. I decided to talk to the chaplain of the church where I was working. It seems a strange choice of where to go to unburden myself, but I've always been fascinated with religion. I was raised Methodist. My mother's family went to church every Sunday, but I don't believe that my curiosity toward religion is spiritual in nature. It never really moved my soul. I am just fascinated with the way people so easily give up their minds and opinions to it. And how they so strongly believe in the boundaries set forth by organized religion. I appreciate the sense of community that people get from belonging to a religious group, and I definitely understand the sense of comfort and safety, though I myself never knew that feeling from a church. When I was a teenager, I used to go to all kinds of churches just to get the experience of different groups. I witnessed people speaking in tongues, and I loved the emotional release I felt when a Baptist congregation was singing and praying. I was quite involved in my church youth group, playing the guitar and even writing religious songs.

But I had a pretty good relationship with the chaplain and trusted he would understand. I explained to him that I had gotten this letter from my mother, and I just put the whole story out there to him. His response floored me. He said, "There are probably some people in this church that would say that it's wrong for you to love another woman. That it's a sin. But I can't go along with them on that way of thinking. I can't believe that God would have

San Francisco, 1983

Christmas in Boston, 1981

La VERANDA

Restaurant

At the Granada Royale Hometel

220 West 43rd — Kansas City, MO 64111
For Banquet Information Call 931-3227

5/31/82

To Whom It May Concern:

Melissa Etheridge entertained in our Westport Connection Lounge for a
seven month period ending May 30, 1982.

Melissa is a very talented performer, versatile with guitar, piano, and
vocals. She is able to perform a wide variety of music, and create and
generate a good audience response. She increased our sales by encouraging
repeat business and by developing a local following.

Melissa was dependable and professional on a business level. She maintained
a consistently good attitude and disposition.

I would highly recommend Melissa as an entertainer in your establishment.
We wish her the very best in her career.

Sincerely,

Patrick Sweeney

Patrick Sweeney
General Manager

*I performed at the Westport Connection Lounge at La Veranda restaurant in
Kansas City until I made enough money to head to Los Angeles.*

invented a love that could be wrong." He encouraged me to get on with my life. He helped me to understand one of the most valuable lessons of my life: to be true to myself. To stand in my truth and be who I am.

I guess the last place I expected to get approval of my feelings was the church. No doubt, a different person could have damned me to hell, but he was really, really supportive, which was fortunate for me. He encouraged me to be who I am. To not shut down my feelings but to embrace them and deal with them the best I could. That was no easy task when I lived in Leavenworth, Kansas, and no easy task as a member of my family. I moved out of the house shortly thereafter. It was the best thing for everyone.

I found an apartment in Kansas City and got a job playing the piano at La Veranda Lounge in the Grenada Royal Hotel. Just like at Ken's in Boston, I got the five to nine slot. The headliners in the nine to one slot were Rhett and Scarlett. There was a gay bar in Kansas City—the Dover Fox, a cute little place. Mixed (both men and women), which you hardly ever got. I dated, saw a couple of women, but nothing serious. My eyes were set on Los Angeles, on fulfilling my dream. Rhett and Scarlett eventually got fired, and I took over the nine to one slot at the Grenada. It enabled me to save enough money to buy a car and get ready for my trip. I started doing some of my own material at the Grenada, which just increased my desire to get discovered, to make a record, to do all those things I'd dreamed about since I was a kid. It didn't happen in Boston. It sure wasn't going to happen in Kansas City. There's only one place to go to do that: Los Angeles. My dream was still in place, still bright and clear in my head. I was about to turn twenty-one and it was time to leave Kansas behind and make the move to L.A. to be a big, famous rock star.

Before I left for Los Angeles, I felt I had one unfinished task that I just had to deal with. I had to tell my father about my sexuality. I wanted to come out to him and be open with him about who I am. I sat him down in the living room, and I said, "Dad, I want to talk to you. I have something I want to tell you. There's something I need to say. I don't know how you're going to feel about it, and I've been afraid to tell you." Blah, blah, blah; I went on and on and on until I finally just came out and said, "I'm a homosexual." My dad looked at me like I was from Mars and said, "Is that all? Well, I knew *that*. It was kind of obvious." He said that although he didn't understand it, if it made me happy, he was fine about it. That was my dad. From then on, his support made a huge difference in how I carried myself about being gay.

Los Angeles

...

A FEW DAYS AFTER MY TWENTY-FIRST BIRTHDAY, I PACKED everything I owned into my car and I drove all alone for four days from Kansas City to L.A. That was a great drive. It was a very liberating experience for me. I was just leaving everything behind. I was driving somewhere I had never really spent any time, and I was going to make a brand-new life for myself. I didn't know what I would end up doing, but I knew that if I was going to make it in the music business, I had to be in Los Angeles. That's where the heart of the music business beats, and I wanted to be a part of that in the worst way. My Aunt Sue lived there and I called her a few days before I packed up my stuff and asked her if I could stay on her couch for a few weeks. She was a little dubious because, as I found out later, my sister had stayed with her in the past. It was a pretty awful experience for my aunt, so she didn't know what to expect when I arrived. But she was great to take me in the way that she did.

The first thing I did after settling in was to start looking for work. There weren't a lot of places for me to play in L.A. This was the early eighties and my sound wasn't exactly what was happening in the music scene at the time. Groups like the Eurythmics, Flock of Seagulls, and Culture Club were on the radio, and I didn't sing, or look, like that at all. Needing money, I auditioned for the Great American Burger Company, a noisy family steakhouse where they had singing waiters and waitresses. I'd never waited on a table before, but I could sing and entertain. The manager of the restaurant auditioned me by telling me to take my guitar over to a table and just start singing. I was supposed to go over to a random table and just sing? Okay. I took a deep breath and I stood in the middle of the room and I began to play. It seemed like the people were enjoying my performance, but they kept right on eating. Out of nowhere, this little girl—she must have been four or five years old—just sticks her tongue out at me. I stared at her for a moment as emotion welled up inside me. But I shoved it down and finished my song. Then I slipped out the side door without saying a word to the manager or anyone. That was *not* what I came out to California to do.

I started to play at a few bars around Los Angeles and Hollywood, but I wasn't really making any money. I was really low and I was at a place where I said, "This sucks." I'd call home and try to sound positive, but it wasn't going quite as I had planned at first. I played at a place called the Candy Store, which turned out to be a black nightclub that had a cabaret. My set list was mostly cover tunes from the sixties, seventies, and early eighties. I'd started off with "Me and Bobby McGee," which got no reaction from the crowd at all. I shifted gears and went into George Benson's "On Broadway." For this song, I'd play the guitar and then hit it, using it to get all the wacky percussive sounds out of it while I was singing. And these crowds loved it. They hooted and hollered and were on their feet. It was always nice to win over a suspicious crowd, but I didn't feel like I was growing with my music. I didn't feel like I was going anywhere.

On the bright side, I was really able to be sexually free in Los Angeles. In fact, I discovered that my father had two gay brothers, George and Carl, who lived in Los Angeles as well. They were very understanding of my sexual preference, completely supportive, and helped me get into the gay community in L.A. When I came out to them, they came out to me. They told me about a bar called Flamingo's, a women's bar that was right down the street from my aunt's house. I started to go there, though I didn't know a soul. I'd sit in the bar all by myself. Every time I think about it, it's just so lonely; but that's what you do in a new city when you're waiting for your new life. Loneliness wasn't powerless. It was powerful. I used it to drive my ambition.

I met a woman who I really liked. I wanted to take her to dinner, but I didn't have any money, so, for forty bucks, I hocked the typewriter I used to type my lyrics on. Then I prayed that the dinner wouldn't be more than that. We went to this Mexican restaurant and, thankfully, dinner was only twenty-four dollars. Only I would hock something to take a girl out to dinner! It's not like I would have done it for myself, but I was only too happy to pawn something that meant a lot to me for the sake of taking this girl out. On our date, I played my demo tape for her. She was totally unimpressed. She put her brother's demo tape in the cassette player, and I was squashed. It was then that I realized I was one of thousands of struggling musicians looking to make it in the business. Up to that point, I was thinking that I was really special. Before I moved to L.A., I was a musician in Kansas City or Boston and I could use my music as a source to impress a woman—you know, help with the seduction—and, for the most part, it worked. But this was L.A., baby, and everyone had a demo tape. That was such a dose of reality. Needless to say, that relationship didn't get very far, but, eventually, I did get my typewriter back.

Not too long after that date, I met a girl named Nancy at Flamingo's. My aunt was out of town, so I decided to bring Nancy back to the house the night we met. Sometimes, when I think about it now, it was kind of creepy that I did that so often, but it never stopped me. In typical Melissa fashion, it was like, "Here we go! I got a new friend." Nancy lived in Long Beach, and when I called her to go on a date, she said, "Come down."

And so, I went down to Long Beach. This was in 1982, and Long Beach was beautiful. It was crisp and clean, bright and beachy. Everybody was tan and it was just *California,* and here I was with the palm trees, the ocean, and a new girlfriend. She had a nice little apartment. I liked that these women had their own apartments and their own lives and their own jobs. Long Beach was really a special time in my life. I definitely think that those were some of my happiest years. I was very free. I was just beginning on my career path. Everything was new. I could be whoever I wanted to be. I was still *me,* but a freer version of myself than I could ever have been in Kansas. I didn't think enough about it to create anybody different, but I knew that, in Los Angeles more than anywhere else, I could be closer to the woman I felt I was on the inside. And then I discovered Long Beach. I could belong to a community. I was meeting new people and making lots of new friends. I had met most of them through my playing at the bars, so everyone thought of me as a musician. I wasn't little Missy Etheridge, the different one, anymore. I was starting to become Melissa. And it felt good.

My first night in Long Beach, Nancy took me to a bar called the Executive Suite. Over in one corner there was a piano, so I asked the manager if they had live music. She said that they did, and she asked me to come back and audition. Of course, I came back on a Sunday and I got the job—five nights a week, playing during the cocktail hour, before the disco opened at night. It was, like, *finally*! There it is, there's my living, and none too soon. I was down to nothing. I had no money left.

Everything I owned was in my car, which made it relatively easy to make the move south to Long Beach. I would stay at Nancy's house. Nancy and I lasted for only a few weeks. Lesbians get serious, like, on the second date, but it was, yet again, a rather complicated situation. I was kind of seeing her, but Nancy was also seeing a guy. I so wanted someone to say to me, "Oh yeah, you're it, boom! That's it, everybody else is gone from my life."

I met another woman and, a few days after meeting her, I packed up all my things, which wasn't much, put them back in my car, and moved in with her. I left Nancy a note. Yeah . . . a note, which was just horrible. She knew that something was going on. I'm so bad at expressing my discomfort. I just close up. I have no tolerance for confrontation; I become emotionless. I just push emotions away. I could feel something for what seemed like a minute and then "Oh no, no, that's not right," and I'd leave and I'd never confront or take any responsibility if there was an issue. I learned this type of response from my family. We just turned it all off. We didn't talk about anything. If there was any type of trouble, we'd sit there and act like it's not happening, and that's exactly what I did as I drove away, leaving my unhappy ex a note on the kitchen table.

Early on in Los Angeles and Long Beach, I used to call my mom from a pay phone and try to tell her that things were going to be fine with me and that she needn't worry. But Mom was always hesitant about my desire to pursue music as a career. Communication was never our strong suit, and I finally sat down to write a song that would express to my mom how I felt about her, about leaving Kansas, and about being in L.A. I never finished it—I couldn't find the right music. But the words were pretty reflective of what I needed to say to her at the time. I still felt that I hadn't won her approval or her unconditional support. Though she's inferred in a few of my songs, I have never written anything other than the following about my mom:

Goodbye, Mother, I realize
You couldn't be here just to say goodbye.
I know you don't approve of a songwriter girl
Leaving to be part of the Rock and Roll world.
If I could ever find a way
To tell you of my dreams
But Mother, someday
They'll be coming to hear me.

Hello, Mother, it's kind of hard to hear you
I'm calling from a booth in L.A.
Right outside a nice fancy club
The lady said that I could play as often as I like
No, Mother, it's just for free
But some even come and listen just to hear me
I'd like to write you
As I'm sure you would me
But we both know how time is.

I found a club in Long Beach, Mother,
The money's not too bad
I found a friend
She shares her house and her life
Even when I lay my guitar to rest
She still wants to hear me.

Father called, said you couldn't really talk
But to tell me hello
And I got the bill yesterday
You forwarded in an empty envelope.

I played last night to a room full of ladies
They know my name, Mother.
A lady hired me
And is paying me a hundred dollars.

She'd never heard me sing
But she knew they loved to hear me
They come from all over to hear
This girl sing.

Yes, they're coming Mother, they're coming
To hear me.
I've got people callin' me
Askin' me to sing
Some to manage, some to design
A girl who's a star in some funny way
Sometimes it's lonely surrounded by smiles.

The woman I left Nancy for was Linda. I met Linda the first night I played the Executive Suite bar in Long Beach, California. These two girls came in and they were very tan. Linda was wearing a white gauze shirt, which showed off the tan even more. Her friend Jill wasn't as tan, but Linda was very tan—beautiful dark skin with long dark hair. She's half Hawaiian, so she's very exotic looking. I was, like, *wow!* It's so funny that their tans are the first things that come to mind when I think about the night we met. I've always had a thing for dark and exotic-looking women. The night we met, Linda and Jill were pretending that they were French— speaking with these really cheesy fake French accents. I knew they were playing around, but there I was, up on this tiny little stage singing, and I thought they were great, especially Linda. I was new to Long Beach and didn't know a lot of people, and they seemed like the kind of women I wanted to know. I was intrigued. At the time, I was staying at Nancy's house. The next morning, the moment Nancy left for work, I called Linda. I went to her house, and we ended up on the couch making love. She was exotic, sexy, feisty, and full of passion.

The two things that she always said about that first day that I came over were: I parked in their driveway (I guess a lot of people, when they first come over to someone's house, will park on the street. What did I know? I was just a girl from Kansas!) and I was looking at the books in her bookshelf, which she claimed really impressed her. She loved that. She's a very literate woman, who was also a writer. Books were everything to her.

Reading was always something that tugged at me from inside. It wasn't the cerebral stuff; it was always the emotional material that I really went for. The same kind of escapism I found in the movies, I easily found in books. There was something about the idea that words could inspire, evoke a response, build up or tear down, praise, destroy. There was an innate understanding of the great power in words. I think that's why reading was my earliest inspiration for writing. I could express myself in the same way that I read other people's expressions of thought and wonder. Happiness and sadness. Loneliness, anger, and desire.

Sometime around the age of twelve, however, I abruptly decided to stop reading. My mother read all of the time, and I guess I felt that she preferred reading her books more than she liked talking to me. By the time I was in eighth grade, I was so envious that her books were getting more attention than I was, I decided that I would never read again. And that lasted until I met Linda. I give her all of the credit for introducing me to books again.

Linda and her friends would play charades, and they'd always use titles to books that I had absolutely no clue about or had never even heard of. Books like *The Brothers Karamazov;* authors such as J. D. Salinger, Kurt Vonnegut, Pablo Neruda, and May

Playing the Executive Suite in Long Beach, California

Playing Vermie's in Pasadena, California

Sarton. I had heard of some of these people but, until I met Linda, I had never read any of them. Reading their words and writings helped inspire my own creativity as a songwriter. I wanted to write smarter. I wanted to be more literary in my approach to lyrics. I wanted them to respect my writing.

Everything happened so fast in our relationship, which is typical for lesbians. Linda was living with her best friend Jill, and I moved in with them practically days after the night we met. You know the joke: What does a lesbian bring on a second date? A U-Haul! That is so true. I never felt the "happily ever after" with Linda. She was one of the women in my life who could never fully commit to our relationship or to me. She always had one foot out the door. I don't think she was unfaithful to me. But, emotionally, she was always limited in what she was willing to give. I believe she felt that she needed to keep her options open, just in case something better came along. She was exciting, and sensual, and attractive. I was living in California, running after my dream, and she filled up a part of that—for a while, anyway.

My emotional range was small when I was living with Linda. I never went into hurt or completely into joy. It was just kind of this in-between feeling. And it was a time for me to learn about myself. Relationships have a funny way of doing that. Every relationship has taught me something about my needs and myself.

There's a certain type of personality that I have been attracted to over the years, but the truth is, with those women, I am not going to find the adoration and sensitivity that I am looking for in a partner. They're women who touch a need inside of me that I've had ever since I was a baby. The need for unconditional love, nurturing, and affection. Linda was a strong personality. She had opinions. She was somebody who had an impact on my life and made a difference. She was a real take-control kind of person. And

I willingly gave that up—for a time. Linda wouldn't come to the bar to hear me play—not very often, anyway—but everybody knew that she was my girlfriend and that I was living with her. But everyone at the bars also knew that I'd have an affair with somebody if a woman came along and lit the fire inside me. It didn't really matter if it was a one-night stand. I'm not proud of that, but that is what it was like for me back then. I was searching. I was always looking for that one person who could satisfy my need. Many have tried. But it has never been enough.

Linda inspired me to start reading again and she opened me up to the idea of pursuing my literary interests. I wanted so much to be smart and articulate and responsible as a knowledgeable person. I wanted to know enough to talk about modern issues and current events. I worked hard to keep on top of all of that, and it inspired me to get more creative and esoteric in my own writing over the years.

Linda and Jill worshiped the poet Carolyn Forché, and I became a fan of hers over the years. Her writings inspired me to try writing in a more bohemian style. The song "Occasionally" was an attempt on my part to be abstract. It is me, really reaching, and trying to be clever in my writing.

OCCASIONALLY

I saw you with your new friends
You wear them so well
Broken shoes and loose ends
Gee you look swell
Me I'm drinking too much coffee
And I'm smoking cigarettes
I'm a deputy of habit
I just can't forget.

I'm only lonely when I'm driving in my car
I'm only lonely after dark
I'm only lonely when I watch my TV
I'm only lonely occasionally.

I saw you with your envoy
A consenting adult
Technique in moderation
But vogue to the cult
Me I've got my strangers
To exile in the night
I guess I'm just addicted
To the pain of delight.

I'm only lonely when I'm driving in my car
I'm only lonely after dark
I'm only lonely when I watch my TV
I'm only lonely occasionally.
Occasionally
Occasionally.

I wrote "Occasionally" in the car. Driving on the freeway in Los Angeles, I kept hearing this rhythm and I was slapping the steering wheel to the beat. The words for the song just came together, right off the top of my head. They tell about a woman I was seeing while dating Linda. The woman came to see me perform in the bar. I had gone out with her a few times, even though we were both in relationships with other women. She walked in with her friends, including her girlfriend. From my perspective, it looked as if she wore her friends like women wear accessories. "I saw you with your new friends, you wear them so well. Broken shoes and loose ends, Gee you look swell." Okay, that's a little abstract, right? I had only been out with this woman a few times, but I liked her a lot, even though I knew the relationship would go nowhere. I was never really a smoker or a coffee drinker (though I drink coffee these days), but I was living in an atmosphere where the women around me were drinking lots of coffee and wine and smoking too many cigarettes, so I knew what it felt like. We were all so tortured and trying to be such beatniks.

I was never alone in those days, but that lifestyle got very lonely at times. Even though I was sharing my life with Linda, I was spreading myself and my affection around to the point where it was becoming thin. I was notorious for one-night stands. Depending on how you look at it, I would meet women, seduce them, conquer, and leave. That was my pattern—and my addiction. It was the idea of complete submission; for a brief moment, this person liked me more than anybody else. It's just a blip on the radar screen, but I'd try to repeat it as often as I could. I never gave one person all of me. Rather, I'd choose to give many women little bits of me at a time, and after a while, I realized that it wasn't the kind of life that would satiate what I really desired in a relationship. It would take me years, and two more relationships, to make that discovery about myself.

Bring Me Some Water

...

Even though I had established a pretty good following when I performed at the Executive Suite, the time had come for me to start playing some other venues. I played mostly women's bars, like Robbie's in Pomona and the Que Sera. They weren't fancy but I always had fun. The Que Sera didn't even have a stage. I'd just stand in the corner of this dark smoke-filled bar and play for the regulars. There was Mary Ellen, the Que's bouncer. We called her Beetle because she had just gotten out of the army. Elsa Benz was the bartender. She would give me such a hard time. There were nights when it was just the three of us in the bar and maybe a few people would come in here and there. Then there were nights when hundreds of people came in and it got crazy. Women were screaming and hollering and drinking and having just too much fun. Of course, there were the four older dykes who, every night, were sitting at the end of the bar snarling at me as I sang too loud and they drank too much. They'd get so mad at me for not playing Dusty Springfield tunes. They crushed me with their indifference.

Sometimes, after performing at the Que, I'd go over to the Long Beach airport, which was a short drive from the bar. There was a road where I could park my car right next to the runway and I would sit and look at the planes taking off and landing. I would dream of someday taking off from there and looking down at the blue lights as we headed up and out over the Pacific Ocean. Of course, in my fantasy, I was always flying off to play some huge arena show. It was within reach, I knew it. I just had to find a way to grab it.

Most people think that I was "discovered" at the Que Sera, but I was actually discovered in a bar called Vermie's, in Pasadena. I had made some fans among a women's soccer team and they came to see me play. There was a woman on the team, Karla Leopold, whose husband Bill was a manager in the music business. My fans on the team dragged Karla to see me at Vermie's one night, after a game, in the hopes that she might somehow convince Bill to represent me. Karla did become a fan, and she promised to get my demo tape to Bill. The word came back quickly from him; he was "remarkably unimpressed." But Karla kept pushing Bill and telling him he had to see me live. When he finally did, he instantly understood my passion for performing. He likes to tell people now that he thought he'd seen the reincarnation of Judy Garland. I don't know about that, but I do know that he was blown away that day and has remained a pivotal part of my career ever since.

Bill took me into the studio to see if he could capture my energy and vibe on tape. Turns out, he could. The recording session took all night. I recorded everything I'd ever written. Solo, just me and either a guitar or a piano. Bill took the tape to every contact he had, to try and get me a record deal. He called the great Clive Davis, thinking that he would surely understand my style, my music, and me—but he didn't. Neither did Capitol, Warner Bros., A&M, EMI, or RCA. Bill kept pushing, but things clearly weren't going to happen overnight.

But L.A.'s a funny place, and opportunities can drop into your lap from just about anywhere. A couple of weeks after Bill signed me, I was in the Que chatting with a girl I knew. She was an agent's assistant in Hollywood and she mentioned that they were casting for the TV show *Fame* and looking for young talented kids. She told me when the cattle call was, so I decided to go. I stood in line all day at the MGM studios as did every other wanna-be-somebody in Los Angeles. I finally get up and sing my song. Three minutes later, I'm outta there. But the next day, Bill calls me to say I've got a callback. Gradually, they winnow it down to ten people who're up for my part. You can't help but get excited about being that close to something. It wasn't making a record, but it was performing. And they were ready to pay something like $3,000 a week—more money than I'd ever dreamed of.

Another callback and it's down to two people: me and some other girl. I go to a recording studio for the final audition. They're doing the screen test, and I get to read with Debbie Allen. Debbie Allen! It was great. And then, in the back of the room, I notice a familiar face. It's Janet Jackson . . . she's the other girl going up for the same part. And right then and there, I knew it was over. I mean, who's gonna get this part: Melissa Lou Etheridge from Leavenworth, Kansas? Or Janet Jackson? After the screen test, Debbie pulled me aside and confirmed what I'd thought. "You know what?" she said. "You're not gonna get this part. I mean, obviously, it's Janet. But don't let this get you down. Don't give up. You are really, really talented. You are going a long way. And you have *got* to keep that dream going." It was really sweet of her because she didn't *have* to say anything other than "Thank you."

Soon after, I was playing Robbie's in Pomona and a woman walked up to me after the show. She shook my hand, and said "I'm Robin Tyler. I run the West Coast Women's Music Festival. Do you want to come play?" Did I want to come play? Of *course* I did. I'd never been to one of the Women's Music Festivals before, much less played at one. But I'd heard all about them. Linda and I drove up to Santa Barbara, and the second I got there I realized that everything I'd heard was true. It was like a football-field-size women's bar. Women were doing everything: lights, sound, performing, everything. And the items that seemed to be least necessary were clothes. I've never seen so much female flesh exposed in one place in my life. Clothes weren't optional for some folks; they were actually frowned upon. It was a great party, and a great audience to play for.

One of the stagehands caught my eye backstage—Kathleen. She was California pretty, with long hair and beautiful green eyes. And she wasn't wearing anything but short shorts and some work boots. Tan all over. And we chatted. And we flirted. And I told her to come down to Long Beach to hear me sing. And she did. We started an affair almost immediately. I'd drive up to her place in Venice, then drive back home to Long Beach and play. Like all of my relationships, things happened fast. It wasn't long before I told Linda I was moving out. I packed up all my stuff and moved in with Kathleen.

If Linda represented my desire to find the kind of love I wanted but never received from my mother, then Kathleen was my version of falling head over heels in love with a woman who represented my father. She was really sweet and fun and nice. I called her "Mother Earth." She was artsy and earthy and extremely laid back. She was the antithesis of Linda, looks-wise. She was fair skinned and had long brown hair. They didn't have very much in common, but Kathleen, like Linda, was completely emotionally unavailable. She wasn't interested in having a monogamous relationship. It wasn't who she was or what she was about. She was really a sixties child. We stayed together for almost four years—some of the best years of my life.

Soon after I moved in with Kathleen, Bill got me a publishing deal with Almo/Irving Music, a branch of A&M Records. It wasn't a recording contract, but it was still huge for me. Signing songwriters just to write songs is a throwback to the pre-singer-songwriter days when there was a line between the artists who wrote the music and the artists who performed the music. But it was a *job,* a job writing music for other people. Basically, I just had this little room with a piano in it, and I'd noodle around on the piano all day, writing songs for myself. Every so often, someone would wander in and ask me to write a song for them—usually for a movie they were doing. *Scenes from the Goldmine, Weeds, Welcome Home, Roxy Carmichel*—a few unknown films from the eighties are floating around with songs of mine in them.

Locked in my little room in Hollywood, I had a lot to write about. My relationship with Kathleen was strong and moving forward, but there was always an unspoken gap between us. We both recognized the gap, and we talked about its existence. But we never talked about how it made us feel. Nonmonogamy was an understood condition of our relationship. It was openly discussed and disclosed. I found myself constantly struggling with feelings of jealousy and anger over it. I have always liked the stability of having and being in a relationship. The thought of one person to come home to is very appealing to me. But I was always having affairs in my relationships before I met Kathleen. Kathleen was the first woman who inspired me to want to be in a monogamous relationship. I had the desire, but she did not. It was strange because I had a hard time accepting whenever Kathleen was unfaithful to me, yet I had no issues with being unfaithful to her. It was never a hidden agenda. . . . I don't know how that kind of relationship can ever really work. It was always filled with such fear, and that fed my insecurities in the worst possible way. I loved Kathleen probably more than I admitted at the time, but toward the end, I was the one who pushed for a committed monogamous relationship—something she simply couldn't give to me.

Do you want to know what comes from a string of nonmonogamous relationships? A bunch of really good songs. I have written so many songs about this subject. I never want to go there again. Lessons lived are lessons learned.

"Bring Me Some Water," "Like the Way I Do," "Don't You Need," and "Similar Features," are each based on lovers' infidelity. Each of the songs speaks to how I felt when my various lovers betrayed me.

"Like the Way I Do" is definitely one of my best songs. It is filled with passion and agony and desire and utter gut-wrenching pain. If you've ever seen me in concert, you know that when I perform that song, it becomes a part of me. It's a transforming song for both the audience and me.

LIKE THE WAY I DO

Is it so hard to satisfy your senses
You found out to love me you have to climb some fences
Scratching and crawling along the floor to touch you
And just when it feels right you say you found someone to hold
*   you*
Does she like I do

Tell me does she love you like the way I love you
Does she stimulate you attract and captivate you
Tell me does she miss you existing just to kiss you
Like the way I do
Tell me does she want you infatuate and haunt you
Does she know just how to shock and electrify and rock you
Does she inject you seduce you and affect you
Like the way I do

Can I survive all the implications
Even if I tried could you be less than an addiction
Don't you think I know there's so many others
Who would beg steal and lie fight kill and die
Just to hold you hold you like I do

Nobody loves you like the way I do
Nobody wants you like the way I do
Nobody needs you like the way I do
Nobody aches nobody aches just to hold you
Like the way I do

I wrote "Like the Way I Do" after Kathleen had told me about someone she had met—someone she hadn't yet slept with but very much desired. She presented me with her intentions, and it fed my insecurities and doubts. At the time, I used to record songs in a makeshift studio at home, using a four-track cassette recorder that I kept in my garage. That kind of recorder could play music backward as well as it was intended to be heard. I had written "I Want You" and was listening to that song. For some unknown reason, I decided to play it backward—I guess to see whether there was some subliminal message in my music that maybe I wasn't even aware of. It was a wacky thing to do, but I really liked the sound. What I heard that day is what became the opening of "Like the Way I Do." The words just flowed from my gut after that, and the rest,

Playing the Women's Music Festivals helped create my early following.

I saw you
on the television
in the television
Headline News
50,000 Fifty Thousand
were ~~the~~ there
And the speaker
And you
Backstage
like I met you
And I fell in love
  Again
I am here having tea
The lid burns my hand
~~5~~ 5000 Five thousand miles away
You are there
And it burns my hand
Will you
Understand
Come home

*A poem I wrote
while Kathleen was
away at the first
march on Washington
for gay rights*

*Kathleen, who
inspired me in so
many ways*

as they say, is history. The power of that song still grabs hold of me every time I sing it. Over the years, I've made it fit to whatever circumstance I've been in. My pride and my ego are wrapped up in all of that gripping emotion. That seeps into the core of who I am—always has. Let's face it. It must have been painful for Kathleen to see me always having these flings. I never gave that much thought in the moment. Of course, I can look back on it now and realize I was no angel myself.

When I write a song from my gut, when I write it from everything deep inside of me, I get such a response, and people know that's where it comes from. It's not that "Like the Way I Do" is such a great song. But it comes right from my center. It burns inside me, and people love that hot place. It's filled with danger and heat and passion and all kinds of untapped fire. This was the first song that coaxed women to come up to me and say, "Play 'Like the Way I Do'" and request one of my original songs over and over. And the more I played it, the better I became at performing it. I save "Like the Way I Do" until the very end of a concert. I let the tension build, and I invite the audience to share the intimacy of the song. I let the fire grow and my passion spills over until I just can't take it anymore and I have to let go . . . and finally, *wham!* "Tell me does she love you, like the way I love you, does she stimulate you, attract and captivate you, does she inject you, seduce you and affect you, like the way I do."

It was so hard for me with Kathleen. Watching her as she drove off to work another Women's Music Festival somewhere, knowing that she would sleep with whoever she wanted to, with no guilt and no qualms. It was a painful place to be in for me. But, on some level, it was exactly the right thing for songwriting. I lived in a constant state of desire and betrayal, and so many of the songs just flowed out.

"Bring Me Some Water" speaks to that same raging passion: my jealousy and fears. The song was a big hit, but it's so riddled with pain. It actually speaks to the double standard I had regarding infidelity. ". . . all in love is fair . . . and I haven't got talking room." We agreed to be in a nonmonogamous relationship. Those were the terms, but somehow I had a much harder time stomaching the idea of Kathleen in the arms of another lover than I had with another lover in mine. It was killing me—her refusal to commit was burning me up inside. That's why I need someone to "Bring Me Some Water." Help me quench this flame. Help me contain my out-of-control fears, insecurities, and wounded heart.

BRING ME SOME WATER

Tonight I feel so weak
But all in love is fair
I turn the other cheek
And I feel the slap and the sting of the foul night air
And I know you're only human
And I haven't got talking room
But tonight while I'm making excuses

Somebody bring me some water
Can't you see I'm burning alive
Can't you see my baby's got another lover
I don't know how I'm gonna survive
Somebody bring me some water
Can't you see it's out of control
Baby's got my heart and baby's got my mind
But tonight the sweet devil, sweet devil's got my soul
When will this aching pass
When will this night be through
I want to hear the breaking glass
I only feel the steel of the red hot truth

And I'd do anything to get it out of my mind
I need some insanity that temporary kind
Tell me how I'll never be the same
When I know that woman is whispering your name

Oh, Devil's got my soul

Sometimes my desires hit a little too close to home. I met a woman in Kathleen's acting class named Jamie, who I was totally crazy about. She was a model-actress who lived in Los Angeles. Jamie was beautiful, sweet, interesting, and smart. She had never been to a lesbian bar nor had she ever been with another woman sexually. There's always been something about women like that that I find so attractive. It's not the idea of "turning" a straight girl; it's more about getting the unattainable. You show me something I can't have and, damn, I want it. I want it right now. Jamie started to come down to the bars to see me play. I'd watch her from the stage as I played and she listened. I'd take her dancing at women's clubs in Hollywood. She used to do this thing where she would turn around and there was a bar on the wall and she would sort of do this dance with the wall. Jamie was very attractive and it wasn't uncommon for men *and* women to just lay themselves at her feet. She commanded that kind of attention. I knew that her curiosity was piqued. We'd meet at Vermie's and the Que Sera, and I opened the door to Jamie having her first gay experience. I would ask her if she was sure that she wanted to go there with me. And she was cautious, but sincere. I would meet her during my breaks, and we would kiss in the back of the bar. We kissed a few times and we'd talk on the phone, but we hadn't slept together. There was always this kind of spontaneous bathroom sex going on in the bars. There is a dark side to my world, and I never wanted Jamie to see the difference. I promised to protect her from the bad part—the fear, the prejudice. She was so brand-new to this alternative lifestyle, she was like wet paint. Fresh and unspoiled. I wanted to be the one who took her for the first time. Eventually, I did sleep with Jamie. We saw each other quite a while. And then the relationship spun. Jamie wanted to get very serious with me, and I was involved with Kathleen. I couldn't fulfill her desire for that kind of relationship. She wanted from me what I wanted from Kathleen, and I just couldn't give it to her. Ultimately, she said that it wasn't working for her any more and that it was time for her to move on. She had met another woman and was seeing her.

The next time Kathleen went to work at one of the Women's Music Festivals, I thought it would be a good idea to give it a whirl with Jamie. No such luck. Jamie completely shut me down. She told me about the new woman in her life, and that was, like, ouch! We had so much fun together, and we used to love to go dancing. We'd laugh the night away. I couldn't have all of the pleasure with Jamie without paying for it in some way. I would have had to give up my relationship with Kathleen and fully commit to Jamie, and I simply couldn't bring myself to do that. There was a rush that came with having an affair, having this secret life. It was too much to handle. You get to a point where you don't want to be having an affair any longer; you want a committed relationship. It's so easy to get caught up in that bliss, that adrenaline bliss, but if you want that from someone who is simply not available, then eventually you have to pull out of the affair for your own good. That's what Jamie had to do. I respect that, and "You Used to Love to Dance" is really an homage to her and that decision—and to my decision to keep on dancing.

YOU USED TO LOVE TO DANCE

Lying in a city night
A million fingers tingling my skin
Out there in the sea tonight
I thought I saw you clutching your sin
You rolled me over long ago
And told me you were strong enough to go
You needed more than this lover's dream
You need the steel and the concrete beams in your life
In your life
We laughed and drank in the jukebox light
And we tore the rug in that downtown dive
Every Saturday night for fifty cents we'd dance all night long
And each new tune we said that's our song
Oh it felt so right

Well ecstasy ain't free
But compromise is chance
I remember how
You used to love to dance

They told me you have found your love
You moved in locked up and put out your blues
Well all God's children got to grow up
And play house make vows to hang up their shoes
Do you sit and talk over coffee cups
Do headline mornings satisfy and fill you up
I kept your eyes and your cigarette kiss
You couldn't keep the lies the adrenalin bliss in your life
In your life

I'm gonna go out tonight
I'm gonna drive up to the hill
I'm gonna dive on into those city lights
And I'm gonna dance, dance
Dance till I get my fill

I was getting paid to write music during the day and paid to play music at night. But it had been over a year now, and there was no recording contract in sight. Sure, there was interest. There's always interest. But the thing about Hollywood is that no one ever wants to say "No." So people would come see me at the clubs. Get all excited and start talking that talk with Bill and me. And then things would just fade away. Interest would turn to silence. It was frustrating. I needed to take that next step in my career. I needed to make a record.

I had decided that if I wasn't signed by the time I was twenty-five, in May of 1986, I was going to just tour America with Kathleen. I was going to call lesbian bars and say, "Hey, it's Melissa Etheridge, you probably never heard of me, but let me come play your bar, I'm traveling through town, let me come and play for fifty bucks." Another friend would come with me, a saxophone and percussion player named Barbara. We were a duo.

Just as we were getting ready to leave, Dino Airali, who worked in promotion at A&M Records, brought Chris Blackwell down to the Que Sera to see me. I had no idea who Chris Blackwell was. So this Brit, dressed in beach pants and flip-flops, walks up to me after my show. And he says, "I'd love to have you on my label. I believe the future of rock and roll has a female face." And I'm, like, "*Cool* . . . but who *was* that?" Turns out that Chris is the founder of Island Records and is responsible for bands such as U2 and Bob Marley and the Wailers. He *got* me for the same reasons that no other record company executive was able to until then. He is a guy who thinks outside the box. Truly a visionary. It was a different time in music. The L.A. music scene was happening with bands like Guns N' Roses and Mötley Crüe. No one was looking for a dark, mysterious rock singer with an acoustic guitar. But Chris could see beyond all of that with me. Through the years, he has been my mentor, my friend, and

Me and
Mary Ellen

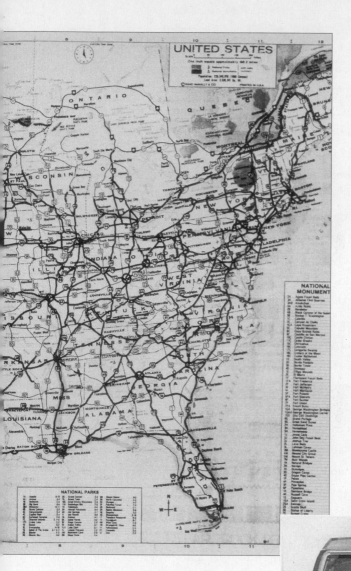

Driving cross-country, performing anywhere they'd let me play. This trip was the inspiration for "You Can Sleep While I Drive."

someone who has always stood by me. He has always spoken the truth with me, and sometimes it was hard to hear, but I have a huge amount of respect for his unedited candor.

The story that has circulated for years is that Chris signed me on the spot that night at the club. Nothing's ever that easy. Chris had to bring some of his A&R people down to see me the next week, to get them on board. After they decided to take me on, we had to deal with the contracts, which could take months. My response was: "Fine, take your time. I've got a tour to do."

The first stop on our journey was Tucson, Arizona. I looked in every gay brochure, found the bars in every town, and called and said, "Hey, do you have live music? I'm coming through." I'd played some Women's Music Festivals, so some places actually knew me. Some people booked me as a real gig in a theater with a couple of hundred people, which was nice. I had my Suzuki Samurai and it was Kathleen; my best friend at the time, Mary Ellen; Barbara; and me. Mary Ellen and Barbara traveled in Mary Ellen's truck. We packed up my own little PA system, a couple of guitars, and Barbara's congas and sax, and we set off on the road. That trip was very free-spirited. I didn't have a record out yet. But we were selling demo tapes that we called "bootleg" at every stop. We went from Tucson to Santa Fe to Texas and New Orleans and Florida. We stayed at Kathleen's friend Barbara's home in Nashville. We played Tallahassee, we played Key West, up through the Carolinas, past New York City, and up into Michigan, where I dropped Kathleen off at another Women's Music Festival. It was getting harder and harder, though, to watch Kathleen in her other life, with all those other women. But those were the rules, right? That's just how our relationship was.

"You Can Sleep While I Drive" is my recollection of that time on the road with Kathleen saying, "Come on, baby, let's get out of this town. Let's do that again." We were really together during those weeks on the road, and I wanted to try and recapture that bonded feeling we shared.

So many people have told me, since then, "What a loving thought: 'You can sleep while I drive.'" Most don't realize that, at the end of the song, the last thing I say is, "Well, if you won't take me with you, then I'll go before night is through"; then you can sleep in your bed, "you can sleep while I drive." Meaning I'm leaving without you. If you're not going to come together with me, I'll go before the night is through, and, baby, you can sleep while I drive. It's funny; a lot of people don't catch that. I've had people come up and say, "Oh, we had that played at our wedding. . . ." I never have the heart to point out the end of the song to them. I just smile and say, "Thanks."

Originally, there was a much longer version of "You Can Sleep While I Drive." It was filled with personal references to Kathleen, to life on the road, and to her fears of completely committing to our relationship. There is no chorus in the song, simply "Baby, you can sleep while I drive." The original version was a little more from the gut and it had a chorus. It started out the same, and there are fragments of the original version in the recorded cut, but take a look at how a song can change over time.

ORIGINAL VERSION "YOU CAN SLEEP WHILE I DRIVE"

Come on baby let's get out of this town
I gotta full tank of gas and the top rolled down
I knew it last night when we were lyin' in bed
You had visions of the highway in your head
I'll pack my bag and load my guitar
In my pocket I'll carry my harp

We'll cross the desert and watch the moon rise
And you can sleep while I drive
I've seen it before this mist that covers your eyes
You'll say that you're searching for something that's not in
    your life
And when the road calls out won't you take me with you
I'll let you sleep while I drive
We got through winter we're sheltered from the cold
We cried through nights and swore we'd never let go
And so the warm weather came whispering your name
And you think of all the lovers you knew
And if I can't go with you I'll go before the night is through
And you can sleep, sleep while I drive.
We'll go through Tucson up to Santa Fe
And Barbara in Nashville says we're welcome to stay
I'll buy you glasses in Texas a hat down in New Orleans
In the morning you can tell me your dreams
Me, I've never been to Montreal I didn't know that you had
I guess you forgot to call
We can stay with your friends no I won't mind at all
I'm sure they'll be glad to see you again
You've had others who shared the miles and your night's bed
I always let you go free just like we said it should be
Loving is hard with wide open arms
I've let you come let you go
Got a good spare brand new stereo
Just washed my car you know she's ready to go
There's nothing here to hold me down
I won't be turning around
And baby you can sleep while I drive
Oh if it's other arms you want to
Hold you the stranger the lover
You're free, why can't you find that with me

On the way back to California, I decided to drive through my
hometown and stay at my parents' house. Every time I'd been back
to Leavenworth since going to L.A., it just seemed to get smaller

and smaller. Other than that, I didn't think this visit would be anything special. Until I saw the package. My contracts with Chris Blackwell and Island Records were finally done. They were waiting for me at my parents' house, waiting for me to sign them. After all the years of playing in bars in Leavenworth, Kansas City, Boston, and L.A., I had a record contract. I was going to make a record. I was so pleased and excited. Everything I'd worked for for years was finally starting to happen.

"Oh My God, That's Me"

...

I T TOOK A COUPLE OF MONTHS AFTER I GOT BACK TO LOS
Angeles, but, finally, things were all ready for me to go into the
studio and record my first album. I flew up to San Francisco with
Craig Krampf, a drummer I had worked with the year before, and
Kevin McCormick, Craig's bassist friend. I'd known these two for
a while—they'd come to see me in the bars—and I felt comfortable
with them. When Island asked me who I wanted to record with,
they were my first choice.

In San Francisco, we met with producer Jim Gaines, who had
produced records for Huey Lewis and the News, Journey, and
Eddie Money—all performers who were hugely successful at the
time. I was ready to listen to Jim and take his ideas to heart. I had
never made an album before, and I wasn't going to act like I knew
more than the experts did. Jim also brought in the keyboard player
from Pablo Cruise. Keyboards were very big in those days; everybody had one. But with ten keyboards and the MIDI setup, it
would sometimes take us all day just to lay down the keyboard

track for one song. It didn't occur to me that layer upon layer of keyboards might not be the best thing for my music. I didn't really think about it; I was so happy to finally be in the studio. I was working hard, putting my music down on record. Kathleen would come visit. When she'd go home, Jamie would sometimes pop up to say hi.

Finally, the album was done. I was a little surprised when I first listened to it. It sounded sorta pop—not how I heard myself at all. Producers want to put their stamp on music albums; Jim's style didn't seem compatible with my sound. Looking back, I realize that I was disconnected from my material. It was like being an artist who gives someone else her paint to use. That person paints a picture with it but then signs the artist's name at the bottom. The album wasn't my picture. It was close, but not me—my vocals, my songs, but certainly not my music. It had been overproduced and had lost its intimate sound. I didn't know there was anything I could do about it, though. I just thought, "Okay, I'm done. Here's the record."

I went to meet Chris Blackwell at the Bel Age Hotel in Beverly Hills to get his reaction to the album. He sat down with me and listened to a couple of tracks. Then he snapped off the tape recorder and looked at me. "I don't like it," he said. I was shocked. He didn't like it? What did that *mean?* Is it all over? Do I just pack up and go home? I walked out of the hotel in a daze, not really sure of what to do. I called Craig and Kevin and told them. "He doesn't like it. Oh, my god. What do we do?" They convinced me to ask Chris for another four days in the studio. "Look," they said. "We know what you need. You just need *us* to be behind you. Just the three of us. Just bass, drums, and you. We'll get this engineer we know, Niko Bolas. He'll just record it raw. He knows what you should sound like."

Photo by Nicole Bengiveno / Matrix

Strong Q⁻

A hold 15ᵗ C᷉ D⁻ C B⁶ D⁻ ?

hey oh hi

_____ like the way I do

Is it so hard, to satisfy your senses

You found out to love me you have to climb some fences

Scratching and crawling along the floor to touch you

(Just when I feel right) / you say you found someone to hold you

does she like I do

    Tell me does she love you

    like the way I love you   don't you think I know there are

    does she ~~cook up too~~ stimulate you   scores of others

    ~~oh~~ attract ~~just to~~ captivate you   who would beg cheat and lie

    does she ~~kiss you~~ just to kiss you   fight kill and die

~~existing~~ ~~oh and kiss you~~ ~~just to~~ kiss you   just to hold you kiss you

    Like the way I do   like I do

    Tell me does she want you

    ~~torture~~ and haunt you

    know just how smoke to touch you

electricity ~~mug you~~ and rock you

    does she ~~chase you~~ inject you

    Seduce you affect you

    like the way I do

~~Is there a reason did you have to give here~~

Can I survive all the rug to others

Even if I tried could you be less than an addiction

So I did. I called Chris and asked him for four days. Four days and we'd re-record the whole album, do it the way it should be done. I promised him it would be that solo girl that he saw and heard in the bars. "That's what I want," he said. "I want the girl in the T-shirt and leather jacket."

So we went back to Cherokee Studios, in Hollywood. Chris came to visit us right at the beginning of the session. He laid down a picture on the mixing board. It was a photo of me standing with clenched fists, wearing jeans, all of my '80s jewelry, a white T-shirt, and a leather jacket, against a red background. That picture would eventually be recreated for the cover of the album. He tapped his finger on it and said, "Make *that* album." I just looked at him, "Okay, Mr. Blackwell." Then Kevin, Craig, Niko, and I got to work. We re-recorded the album. Four long days and four longer nights, but we made *my* first album. It was such a different experience this time. The four of us were just *in* it, all day and all night. I brought in "Bring Me Some Water," which I had just written, and they came up with the whole thing behind it. It was exactly like it should have been. Everything just clicked.

I brought the new album to Chris, and he loved it. All except "Like the Way I Do." He thinks I'm sorta hollering on that song. "Don't like that one," he says. Those four days in the studio had really enlightened me about how I wanted to sound on a record. I was much more sure of myself after that experience. "No, Chris," I replied. "That's my favorite song. It stays." Chris just shook his head. "All right, if you have to." To this day, whenever Chris gives me an opinion on what to keep and what to get rid of on an album, he inevitably brings up that he didn't want "Like the Way I Do" on my first album. But the final cut is always up to me. One footnote to the album-cover story. When the photographer was taking the photo of me that was eventually used—a match to the one Chris

Recording
"Never Enough"

Performing during my
first American tour

My mentor and friend,
Chris Blackwell, who gave
me my first recording deal,
with Island Records

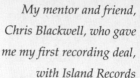

The "first" first-album
song list

On the train in Europe,
during my first tour

had held up when he said "Make this album"—I was dancing to
"Like the Way I Do."

So the album was done and I was on my way, right? Nope. In
the music industry, nothing ever works the way you'd like it to.
They put off the release date for a few months, and I just had to
wait. I went back to playing the bars, back to my old life. Things
were going okay with Kathleen, but I wanted to make my mark,
and all I could do was wait.

Luckily, Bill got me a job on a European tour—opening for
Martin Stevenson, a folk-rocker from Newcastle, England, who had
a huge Jimmy Stewart obsession. It was my first time in Europe
and my first real rock-and-roll tour. On the bus with ten other
people; roadies; a new city every day—it was exciting and boring,
terrible and wonderful, all at the same time. I'm walking on stage
in front of people who have no idea who I am. They don't know me
from Adam. Sometimes I win them over. I can see people nodding
their heads, smiling, giving me an "Oh, she's *good*" look. And, of
course, sometimes I don't win them over, I'm just out there doing
my thing and the audience is just biding its time, waiting for Martin.

The album wasn't out yet, but the record company in England
was trying to garner support for it. I was in the back of a car, being
driven crazily through the streets of London to try to make a train,
when "Similar Features," the first single off the album, came on
the radio. It was shocking. "Oh, my god! That's *me*!" I'd never
heard myself on the radio before. I broke down in tears, right in the
back of the car. Just completely cried when I heard that song. *My*
music pouring out of that tiny radio in the front of the car. And it
sounded so good. It sounded great! I was just overwhelmed.

The tour sure wasn't the rock-and-roll big time. It was dreary
little hotels with the bathroom down the hall. And it wasn't like we
played London. We were in Leicester and Birmingham and Leeds

and Glasgow, and all these little working-class towns. I'd work all night and then do press all day. The English tabloid press was asking me oddball questions. "What's it like growing up in Kansas?" "Your songs are very painful. Have you had your heart broken a lot?" "Have men always treated you badly?" That was always the hard one. They assumed I had relationships with men, and, not being out of the closet at all, I just answered by talking about "relationships," never, ever, being gender-specific.

And it was lonely—really, really lonely. When I got to the Continent, I couldn't understand a word and didn't have anyone to talk to. When I wasn't working, I'd just wander around these strange, ancient cities and look around. This was in the days before AT&T phone cards. I had no idea how to call home. So I'd just sit in whatever hotel room I happened to be in, and write.

I wrote a lot of songs that have gone on to become favorites of my fans over the years—songs such as "The Angels" and "Royal Station 4/16." All of them were written in various hotel rooms throughout Europe. The common theme was that overwhelming sense of loneliness I felt on the road. I was still in my relationship with Kathleen, and that was in trouble. She was still fighting a committed relationship, which, for me, seems to be a recurring nightmare. In songs like "The Angels," I wrote weepy pining lines like, "All I want is for your love to be all mine but the angels won't have it." That's just something I felt I'd never have. It speaks to that big, dark, deep, empty place in my heart. "Sometimes I feel like an innocent one to deserve this fate, what have I ever done?" I was writing specifically about this relationship but talking very generally about the emptiness that I felt. I just wanted someone to say, "Yes, I love you and only you and I'm here and we'll walk side by side. You work on you and I'll work on me, and I'll catch you when you fall and you catch me when I fall." That's all. It seemed so simple to me, but because of the tracks that have been laid, I can't seem to get there.

When I was in Germany, I went to Dachau, a concentration camp that had been turned into a Holocaust museum. It's a devastating experience to see a concentration camp that is, for the most part, pretty much as it was left after the end of the war. It's like a museum, but with the worst possible collection of memories.

There are all kinds of memorials around the camp, in honor of those who died. As we were leaving, a man was standing outside the gate and passing out flyers. I read the paper he handed me. It said that the people who run Dachau would not allow a memorial to the homosexuals who died there. I was shocked by what I read. I sat down and wept. I couldn't believe it. I thought about the civil rights bills that have been passed over the years to protect all sorts of groups but still won't include the word *homosexual*. We live in a society that's all wrapped up in its Puritan ways.

I was standing on the site where this horrible atrocity happened, and everywhere I looked there were reminders that we must never let it happen again, but nowhere did it acknowledge that, along with the six million-plus Jews who died in the Holocaust, homosexuals were also persecuted and tortured and put to death. The uniforms with pink triangles hang right beside the ones with the yellow stars of David. But, when I was there, no memorial had been erected to honor those who wore those pink triangles. The symbol we view today as a positive image for homosexuals was actually a way to identify and exterminate gays during the war. It was the first time I had a recognition of myself as a lesbian in relation to the rest of society. As hard as parts of my life were because of being gay, I actually had a pretty easy time. I always found support; my family never rejected me. I had never lost anything because of my sexuality. And here I was, standing in front of a place that had executed people just because they were gay. It was a powerful moment. A defining realization.

The flip side of my experience at Dachau occurred a few years later, in Berlin. Days prior to my Berlin show, we were hearing news stories of people fleeing East Germany and risking their lives. At first we weren't sure that we should even go to Berlin. We feared there might be trouble. My tour manager at the time, who was German, assured me that if there were any signs of trouble, we'd leave. We drove our tour bus overnight from Hanover, in West Germany, and I fell asleep. When I awoke the next morning, the bus was stopped. I got up and looked out. We were in a sea of cars filled with East Germans driving into West Berlin. Under political pressure during the night, East Germany had opened the gates through the Berlin Wall. There was truly an electric feeling in the air as we arrived.

I went to the Wall and stood there with thousands of people. Unarmed soldiers were standing on top of the Wall that first day. I witnessed a five-year-old girl run up to the Wall and hit it with her tiny little fist in defiance. That night, the soldiers came down, and so did the Wall . . . literally.

The next day, there was a free concert for the East and West Berliners, and I got up on stage to perform very unexpectedly along with Joe Cocker and some German bands. I could tell the West Berliners from the rest of the crowd because they had experienced a rock concert before and were loose and having a great time. The East Berliners just stood there with their mouths wide open. They had never seen anything like this. It was completely overwhelming. My concert later that night was very spirited. It was an amazing part of history, and I'd say that most people in attendance were high on freedom. It was very inspiring and very hopeful. I felt very honored to have witnessed this historic change firsthand.

The tour with Martin Stevenson ended and it was time to go home. Home to my friends, *my* life, Kathleen. Kathleen. I had missed her so much while I was away. I was really starting to feel the need for commitment. For a life together that was really *together*, not always focused on running away for private moments with other people. But it was hard. After all, I had an album coming out. And I was going to go on the road. I was gonna make all those Rock Star dreams come true.

Julie

...

WHEN I GOT HOME, THERE WAS A PACKAGE WAITING FOR me—a brown box. I opened it up and there was the record. *My* record. The album and a 45 of "Bring Me Some Water." The single and the album were all red and black. Everything was red and black. And I just stared at it. Touched it. It was amazing and delicious and wonderful. I could have eaten it. There it was. My record.

You make a record and you're supposed to go on tour to support it. And that's exactly what I did. Kevin came with me to play bass, but Craig was afraid of flying, so we hired Fritz Lewak to sit in as the drummer. It wasn't like the European tour, though. It was much better.

I had my own tour bus. My own roadies. People working for me, taking care of me. This was *my* tour. The second stop we made was in Kansas City, Missouri, at the Lone Star. All of my friends from Kansas City and Leavenworth came to see me play. It was great—all my friends dancing and partying, my mom and dad sitting at a table in the back, nodding their heads to the music. Even

Jennifer came, though she spent most of the evening in back of the bar, drunk. This was *my* tour. It felt so . . . legitimate. My band. My music. I wasn't doing covers. I wasn't playing in the corner in a women's bar. I was playing in a club where people had paid to see *me*. That night, we drove to St. Louis, where I was going to make my first music video.

I got to the club—the Mississippi Nights, where we were going to film the "Bring Me Some Water" video—first thing in the morning. I was introduced to the first assistant director, who looked at me and said, "Hello, my name is Julie Cypher." All I could say was, "Well, hello." She was the most beautiful, powerful, sexy woman I had ever met. She was a perfect assistant director; she kept things moving, on time and on schedule. I was instantly crazy about her. I flirted and played and sang and used all of my talent and charm to get her attention. When we were introduced, there was an instant, very real, deeply intense connection between us.

The next day, Julie came over and said to me, "You know, my husband knows someone that knows you." All I could hear was the word *husband*. My heart sank. I had never thought about husbands before. They hadn't really been a part of my world up to that point. I was crushed. Julie's husband was the actor Lou Diamond Phillips. They had gotten married very young. I met her when she was twenty-four. I was twenty-seven at the time. As I was saying goodbye, I shook everyone's hand to thank them for their assistance with the production. When it came time to say goodbye to Julie, I put my arms around her and gave her a hug. She whispered softly in my ear, "If I wasn't married. . . . "

I was inspired and confused. I didn't know what to think. All I knew was that I couldn't get this girl out of my head. Two weeks later, I was in Toronto doing a sound check for my show that night, and I turned around to find Julie, with her very famous actor-husband, standing there in the auditorium. My heart was pounding. I could feel it beat against my chest so hard, and I hoped that they wouldn't notice. We talked like old friends and decided to all go out to dinner together with my band. We were all sitting at the table together, and Julie was sitting right next to me. I couldn't actually flirt with her; her husband was right there! But we talked and we laughed and we had a great time. But it was odd. I had such feeling for this woman and didn't know where to put it, what to do with it. As she was leaving, Julie handed me her phone number, and I slipped it into my pocket.

Julie went back to L.A. and I went to Montreal, where I stared at her number for days. And then I called Kathleen. I asked her, for the final time, if she thought that we could ever be in a monogamous relationship. And for the final time, she said, "No." It just wasn't what she wanted. I hung up the phone and then called Julie. We talked for hours. We fell in love on the phone. We got to know each other through endless conversations while I was on the road and she was at home alone while Lou was making a movie. It was all so new for both of us. I felt like I could tell Julie anything and everything. It all felt so right and real and possible. We talked every night for hours and hours. I remember one night when Julie called me in New York City and she said, "We have to stop meeting like this."

We'd only been talking on the phone, but it had gotten intimate. I felt so close to her, I knew that there was something more than conversation growing between us. It had gotten so personal that Julie was beginning to feel guilty. I had invited her to meet me in Dallas for a few days while I was there to do a concert, and even though I knew she had her hesitations about making that trip, she came to see me.

We danced, drank, and had the greatest time. That was all. Julie would not kiss me. I, of course, was perfectly respectful of her fidelity. But there was no doubt that there was a special feeling between us. Shortly after that trip to Dallas, I invited Julie to come up to Vancouver at the last minute for the last show of my first American tour. It was a big deal to me, and all of the band members were inviting their girlfriends, so I asked Julie if she wanted to come, too. I reassured her that it was just as friends and that I'd arrange for her to have her own room. My tour manager then informed me that there were no other hotel rooms available, so I called Julie back and promised that I would be on my best behavior and that she could stay in my room. I even offered to get her a room at another hotel, but she thought it was fine and said that she was in. She flew up to Vancouver and I did the show. There was all of the sexual energy between us, but Julie was still very much married. We got ready for bed that night, and Julie came out wearing these boxer shorts and a *Young Guns* T-shirt. *Young Guns* was a Western that her husband had starred in. And the picture on the T-shirt was of Lou staring and pointing a gun straight at me. I don't think Julie put on the shirt consciously, but I just had to laugh inside. I was like, "Okay. I'm not going to touch you, I swear!" But it wasn't easy . . .

The next day, we took a ferry from Vancouver to Victoria. Victoria is especially beautiful in October. It's really sweet up there. The leaves were magnificent—at the height of changing colors— and they were falling everywhere. We walked around Victoria and found this beautiful old building with these magnificent grounds. There was a huge pile of leaves, and Julie jumped right in there and started rolling around. We had the best time on that trip. A year later, after we became a couple, Julie gave me a frame she had made. Mounted inside were some leaves she had taken and saved

This photo was taken on the day I met Julie, while shooting my first video. That's John Shanks behind me.

Two years later, in Victoria, British Columbia

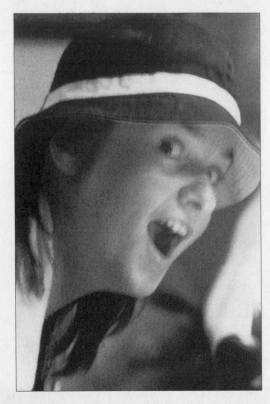

Turning twenty-five. I wished for a record deal...

Celebrating my thirty-seventh in Santa Fe

from that gloriously wonderful day in Victoria. I still have that frame in my house.

A couple of days after returning to Los Angeles, I stopped by to see Julie at her house in Laurel Canyon. I was on my way home from an appointment. It was a hot day and she had a blue summer dress on. We were just sitting and talking. Suddenly, she leaned over and kissed me. It was one of those perfect kisses. We slipped onto the floor, still locked together. It was a very serious kiss. I was confused yet again, but also delighted and deliriously happy. We made plans to see each other later that day at my house, before my show at the Roxy that night. Then I left. I probably looked really stupid as I drove down Laurel Canyon with a big, goofy grin on my face.

In the world of rock and roll, especially in Los Angeles, playing the Roxy is a really big deal. I dreamt of playing the Roxy when I first moved to L.A., and I had opened for Lyle Lovett there before my first record was released. Playing it again as the headliner was a big moment for me, so I had a preshow party at my house for all my friends who were going to the show. I was still living with Kathleen at this point, and while the party was going on around me—all my friends, Julie, Kathleen, the show at the Roxy—I just felt *alive*, like all my senses were on full alert. The mystery, the intrigue, the excitement took that Grandma's-coconut-cake feeling to a whole new level. Eventually, everyone left the party, and Julie and I were alone, standing in my backyard, talking. Just like earlier in the day, she stepped right up and kissed me. It felt so good to lose myself in her. To sense the promise of what we might have together . . .

Needless to say, the show at the Roxy rocked. Only four hundred people were there that night, but, I swear, thousands have come up to me over the years and said they were there the night *I* played the Roxy. It was a magical moment in my career. Both Julie and Kathleen were there, but I played to Julie all night long. When it came time for "Like The Way I Do," I sang it straight to Julie, pouring it all out for her right there. I have no idea if Kathleen noticed or not, but I must have been pretty obvious. I got completely lost in that performance, and I wanted to give all of me to that night, that show, and that woman.

It was that second kiss, which was a really good kiss, that was the inspiration for "Must Be Crazy for Me." Even though Julie had kissed me the first two times we kissed, she was also sending me very clear signals that she did not want to have a relationship with me. Every time we connected or I tried to get close to her, Julie would run away from the situation as fast as she could. I would make a move, slide closer to her, and she would tell me to take my thigh off of her. She kept shutting me down, which was a clear sign that she must really be crazy for me, right? Although I didn't have the self-esteem to write this song *in* the moment, I did write it *about* the moment, after Julie and I had finally united as a couple. Admittedly, "Must Be Crazy for Me" is a bit of a cocky song, but that's who I was in those days. It was deliriously fun.

MUST BE CRAZY FOR ME

You tell me not to call you up
Cause it ties you down
Don't tell your friends
You've been hangin' round
You must be crazy for me
You say you'll see me once or twice
Every week or two
There's more important things
That you've got to do
You must be crazy for me

Cause when I kissed you last night
In my own backyard
You ran so fast
And you fought so hard
You must be crazy for me

You must be crazy for me
You don't like my hair
You don't like my car
You don't like my friends
You met at the bar
You must be crazy for me
I see you shake your head
And you roll your eyes
Your firm remark
To remove my thigh
You must be crazy for me

Do not expect you to wait
Do not expect you to phone
Do not expect anything
When I catch you alone
You must be crazy for me

I left to tour Europe not too long after that, and I really wanted Julie to meet me in Switzerland. I had a few days off, and I wanted to spend them with her. I was elated when she said that she would join me, but she made it clear to me that she was still struggling with her marriage and just wanted to be friends. That was hard for both of us because we were feeling so uncertain about what was happening. We were absolutely perplexed by the dilemma our emotions were placing us in.

I met Julie at the airport and we took a train back to Lausanne, where we stayed at this small, charming hotel in a vineyard right by the train station. We walked around the city and drank cappuccinos and ate *éclairs de chocolat*, and we got to know each other on a different level—in person together; not with the boundaries of a telephone between us. That night, after a lot of deliberation and trepidation, we made love for the first time. It was incredible. It was emotional and loving and sexy and everything I had dreamed it would be. We left Switzerland and went to Rome and then to Stockholm. It was a wonderful, beautiful, magical time for both of us.

I was smitten. I definitely thought that this was it. I was going to settle down. Here we go. After my string of nonmonogamous relationships, I was completely ready to have a loving one-on-one love affair. Before Julie left Europe, I told her how I felt and that I thought she needed to go home and tell Lou what had happened. I didn't want to have an affair. I wanted to make a life with her. It wasn't an easy conversation. As hard as it was for me, I am sure it must have been even harder for Julie to have to go home and face telling her husband that not only had she had an affair, she had had it with a woman. I suggested to her that she seek therapy to help her understand what was going on inside her head and with us, and why this was happening. I have been in therapy for many years, and I really believe that it's a fabulous way of breaking through those walls in one's life and understanding the detours on the road that suddenly seem to come out of nowhere.

When I met Julie, she most certainly had not been with any other women; as far as she let me know, she had never even thought about it. Because she had married Lou when she was twenty-two years old, she hadn't even had that many relationships. She went back to Los Angeles and tried to make her marriage work. She told her husband everything, but the marriage couldn't survive. I don't think that it failed because of our liaison. I think that it suffered from what damages many young marriages: There wasn't enough communication or understanding about relationships and life.

Before Julie divorced Lou, we all tried to maintain some kind of friendship together—as strange and as awkward as it seems, looking back on it now. Lou finally got to a point where he had to just emotionally check out of the relationship. It was clear that their marriage was not going to work, and he was well aware of my feelings for his wife. Julie tried to keep everything amicable for everyone involved. She's very much that way. She's the kind of person who can stay friends with her ex-lovers. Even after she had left Lou and we were openly dating, we tried to see him occasionally. He had a Texas blues band that he played in, and we'd all get together and jam. Whenever I'd ask him how he was doing, he'd only talk to me about business. We kept this going for a few months after their breakup, but he was slowly moving away from the situation, and I can understand that it must have really been hard for him. I think that it became too painful for Lou in the end, and he ultimately closed that door.

A year after we made love for the first time, Julie filed for divorce. I was genuinely sad for her and Lou's failure. I had considered him a friend, but I was so happy about our being able to come together. It was everything I had ever wanted. I said good-bye to Kathleen. I said good-bye to Jamie. I left my past, and all of the patterns that had gotten me to this place, behind me. This was going to be my true love. The one I had waited for my entire life.

When people ask Julie about how she fell in love, she always says that she fell in love with my soul, with me as a person. Gender simply was not an issue. Whatever our dysfunctions were, something clicked between us and worked for us.

I was anxious to finally have this relationship that I had always dreamed of—the movie fantasy—so I was probably very demanding in the beginning. I had been through the dating thing, and I wanted no part of that world anymore. I had found the love of my life. When Julie and I met, I felt, for the first time, that I wanted to clean up my act and be committed. I wanted to make the relationship all about her. (Later, I would discover that this was not a good idea. You can never make a relationship work if it's all about only one of the partners.)

Finally, I'd found the relationship that I could commit to, the relationship to be monogamous in. Even (and this was a radical thought in those days) the relationship to raise children in . . . I think Julie might have preferred to date some other people before we really settled into our relationship. Men or women or both. But we were devoted to each other. And, for a while, that was enough.

Brave and Crazy

...

Aﬀter my first tour ended, I went right back into the studio to rehearse the songs that would become my second album, *Brave and Crazy*. I was still working with Kevin McCormick and Fritz Lewak. We had a rehearsal studio in North Hollywood. Someone comes in to tell me I've got a phone call, and I walk down the hallway to the pay phone. Bill is calling. He says "Are you sitting down?" I laugh because that's always what Bill says, and I'm never sitting down. "You've been nominated for a Grammy." I *should* have been sitting down. What he'd said was so completely out of left field! There wasn't one thought in my head about actually being nominated for a Grammy Award. I mean, I'd done okay. I'd been on some radio stations, sold some records, but it wasn't like I was on my way to becoming a superstar. I hung up the phone and instantly told everyone I knew. It was such a rush.

I was nominated for Best Female Rock Vocal Performance, up against Sinead O'Connor, Toni Childs, Pat Benatar, and Tina Turner. It was such an honor, so completely out of nowhere. And not only was I nominated, but I was going to get to perform on the show too! It was the year of Tracy Chapman, and there was this bill of female artists, so they decided to showcase us. Which I sure wasn't going to complain about.

I flew in from my gig in San Francisco the night before, so I was ready to go. I was still with Kathleen at this point, so, of course, she was my date. There was an odd moment when we first arrived because it suddenly became clear that they'd show us on camera as the awards were being announced. Bill pulled me aside and told me that he'd like to sit next to me. For a moment, I was frozen. Did he want to sit next to me because he deserved it as much as I did? Which, of course, he did. Or was it to camouflage the fact of my sexuality in front of a television audience? I didn't know. But Bill's my manager and I loved him, so of course I said yes.

Walking in, though, I had no idea what to expect. How could I? I'm sure I had this wide-eyed glaze that everyone has their first time. There were so many people there who I admired, who'd influenced me over the years. I was definitely a little starstruck. Of course, I didn't win, Tina Turner did, but that didn't really matter. After all, I was gonna play, right?

I remember Billy Crystal introducing me as I was standing backstage. I was so wired, so filled with expectation and emotion and nerves and desire . . . it was just like doing the Bob Hammill Variety Show for the first time, only multiplied by a hundred. I wasn't playing to a big room or an arena. I was playing to sixty million people!

So I did. I went out there and did "Bring Me Some Water," and I felt huge. Like I was on fire. Like I was playing my heart out. I looked out at the audience . . . and no one was moving. Nothing. Only Stevie Wonder bobbing his head a bit as he listened. It was a huge surprise. I mean, I'm used to people moving when I play and this was just . . . nothing. They just sit there at the Grammies. It's got to be one of the hardest places on earth to play. It's just horrible. So I looked right at Stevie and played the whole thing to him. I finish, and there's this huge round of applause. I guess they liked it, but they sure didn't show it at the time. The next day, there was a huge jump in my record sales. Something like 60,000 records, all over the world. That performance, I think, was instrumental in setting the stage for the growth of my career.

I went to the party afterward with Kathleen, and met folks like George Harrison and Tom Petty, which was great. Then I spotted this gal in the corner, just a cowboy girl head to toe, with this harsh buzz haircut. And she was standing there with what was clearly her girlfriend. So Kathleen and I slide on over there and start chatting with k.d. lang and her girlfriend. K.d. and I instantly hit it off. Though there was never a physical connection between us, we always had a great time together.

After the Grammies, I went back on the road. Practically doing nothing but touring and waiting for the fallout between myself and Kathleen, and Julie and Lou. When I finally got back to L.A. six months later, things had been resolved. Julie had left Lou, and Kathleen had moved to Atlanta. Getting off the road was great. Julie and I could finally spend the kind of time together that we needed.

K.d. lang was in L.A. for a while and stayed at my house. The first time Julie met k.d., she was very intrigued and seemed to be immediately attracted to her. I think there was this door that had been opened within Julie. It made her feel like she needed to better understand what it meant to be involved in a relationship like ours. I believe she felt that in order to *have* the experience, she wanted to *know more* about the experience. That's Julie. She's intense, smart, inquisitive, and strong. How could I not understand her curiosity? I didn't like it, but I felt at the time that I had to accept her request. Julie said that she had developed a strong desire for k.d., and, in a very truthful way, she told me she wanted to sleep with k.d., which completely shook the foundations of my world, bringing up all my issues and insecurities. My deeply intense emotions were completely assaulted. I was unaccustomed to talking about infidelities *prior* to anything actually happening. My history was to deal with it after the fact, if at all.

Since I was the first woman Julie had ever been with, she was curious to know whether she was attracted to other women. She came to me and said that she would like to experience another woman. This had been a common theme throughout my past relationships, and I really did not want it with my new love. The women I had been involved with prior to Julie, though they were very close relationships, they were definitely not monogamous. Even though I believed an "open" relationship was a good idea at the time, it always hurt me when past girlfriends went out with someone else, and I carried that pain into my relationship with Julie, whether I was aware of it at the time or not. Of course, it never seemed to bother me quite as much when *I* went out and did it. What a double standard. But Julie was the first woman I never wanted to have an affair on. I so wanted to be committed. Her to me and me to her.

So here comes Julie, openly explaining her wish to be with someone else, and then totally reassuring me that she still loves me and that this desire doesn't mean that she wants to leave me. What was I supposed to do with that concept? That was a first for me. I was angry, jealous, hurt, and confused—not just with Julie, but also with k.d. I selfishly pleaded with Julie to not go through with it. I wanted her all to myself. I looked at our relationship as a precious physical sharing of sexuality that was supposed to be only between Julie and me.

Somewhere inside of me, my ego was terrified and lost and broken down, but I felt that I couldn't deny this person I loved so much an experience she wanted to have for herself. Looking back on it now, I probably feared losing Julie if I didn't support her desire. It became obvious to me that, once again, I had selected a partner who was not ready to settle down when I was ready. I didn't want to lose my relationship; I was completely in love with her. Inside, I was pleading, "No, no, no! Please don't do this to me, to us, to our relationship." As strongly as I felt, I somehow understood that I wasn't going to lose Julie over this. But in the same breath, I knew that I would never really have all of her either. And interestingly, after that experience, Julie never saw k.d. again—at least not in *that* way. We still see her socially from time to time, but the friendship has never really been the same.

It took me a long time to get over the incident with k.d. A part of me tends to drown in those feelings even after all of these years. I wrote a few songs about that encounter. I never wanted to go through that again with Julie. I wasn't mad at k.d.—okay, maybe I was a little—but we have put it long behind us. We spoke about it once, over the phone. I just said to k.d. that I thought that it sucked that this was going on between her and my girlfriend. I felt, like, kind of stupid about the whole thing. It's not that particular incident; it's the idea that Julie could never commit to me and only me. As I've said so many times already, monogamy was never something I wanted in a relationship *before I met Julie.* But something clicked when I met her. I wanted her and only her. As far as I'm concerned, I haven't looked at another woman for ten years. She was the only person I could see, the only woman I wanted, and definitely the woman I needed in my life, if even to a fault.

A couple of years later, I was sitting in a hot tub with Ellen DeGeneres, k.d. lang, Julie, and a couple of other women, and we were going around the tub asking each other to say a word that described each of us. When it was k.d.'s turn to describe me, she said, "Generous." I think she was saying that she thought I was very generous to open up that part of my relationship with my partner to someone else. I didn't look at it that way, although I appreciated the gesture on k.d.'s part.

I have always believed that love is dramatic and emotional. I believed that the world worked like this: You fall in love, you're committed, and you live happily ever after. In the movies, actors always have the right thing to say at exactly the right time. (If only someone would give me the script to my own life.) For me, writing music has been my best way of expressing how I feel. It has taken me a lot of years to realize that how I feel about a particular circumstance is as important (if not more so) as how someone else is feeling. I constantly have to remind myself of that.

Ultimately, what happened with k.d. was exactly what Julie had said it was going to be, an experience to help her better understand her own feelings. But I carried all of my issues about relationships, love, mistrust, mindsets, and psychological sex with me during that incident. To me, sex is as much about your mindset as it is about your body. It's about the dance and seduction and the conquering, the having—and yes, the winning. Sex is very dark to me in that way, and yet, for Julie, this experience wasn't about that at all. It was about her body. Her physical attraction. Afterward, we talked about her experience, and I asked her all of the horrible and painful questions I did and didn't really want to hear the answers to. I wanted to know everything. We managed to get through the experience and actually became closer than ever. The lesson for me in all of this was that I learned to really trust Julie. With her, what you see is what you get, and knowing that was important to me. After all that had been dealt with, Julie and I decided that it was time to move our relationship to a new level. We decided to move in together.

We found a sweet little house in Hollywood. It was small and cozy and perfect for two people in love. The years that Julie and I lived in that Hollywood house were probably my very favorite days together. We had moved beyond the k.d. situation and had finally decided to make our relationship official. It was just a great time. Everybody we were hanging out with was new to Hollywood. It was a constant social gathering. There was this young actor named Brad Pitt who had just made a movie called *Thelma and Louise,* and who was learning how to fly-fish in our pool for a movie called *A River Runs Through It.* He hung out with this really cute boy named Dermot Mulroney and his then-girlfriend, Catherine Keener. Dermot played the cello on the song "Place Your Hand," off of the *Never Enough* album. There was this really funny girl named Rosie O'Donnell who was working for VH1, and my friend Ellen, an up-and-coming comedienne. Even k.d. lang was around the house from time to time. Julie was starting her movie, *Teresa's Tattoo,* which she was directing. (We all had cameos in it.) We were all struggling, just trying to make our dreams come true in Hollywood. There were lots of talented writers, actors, and producers all waiting to make the big time. It was a very sweet and innocent time. Those years are the ones that I look back on and think of most fondly.

When the riots happened in Los Angeles, everyone came up to our house and stayed the night. It was a refuge. We climbed up on the roof and just watched L.A. burn. As upsetting as it was, it was a comfort to us all to be together.

We've all come a long way since hanging out together, and, as a result, we don't get to see each other as often as we would like. I'm glad that we shared those times together, because things have a way of changing. There's no way they stay the same. If they stayed the same, we'd all still be starving artists just starting out, wanting more.

Talking to My Angel

...

AFTER *BRAVE AND CRAZY*, IT WAS BACK OUT ONTO THE road and then back into the studio to start my third album, *Never Enough*. Those were the years when I really had the fire inside me. To perform, to produce, to love Julie. I was so filled with a hunger and a desire to succeed and move onto the next level—I was just driven. I just wanted to go, go, go.

I was still working with Kevin and Fritz. Kevin was becoming a part of my musical growth. We actually produced *Never Enough* together. We were in the studio working one afternoon when I got a phone call from my parents. It was one of those phone calls that you just never want to get. My dad had just been diagnosed with inoperable liver cancer. I couldn't handle this in our usual family way. I couldn't just pretend this wasn't happening.

The first phone call I made was to my manager, Bill. I was sobbing uncontrollably, and Bill did what he does best with me. He went into a protection mode. He assured me that I had his total support to do whatever I needed to do to get through this, and said that I need not worry about anything else other than taking care of my dad. Bill took care of rearranging all of my business obligations, and he made space in my schedule so that I could bring my parents out to California and get my dad the very best medical attention available. Bill was my rock throughout the whole cancer ordeal with my father. But that's Bill. He is strong and smart and supportive and loves me completely without condition.

When my parents called, they told me that my father had anywhere from six weeks to six months to live. Knowing that L.A. had great cancer centers and, more importantly, wanting to be near my dad, I brought my mother and father out to Los Angeles to see what could be done. Waiting for them at the airport, I couldn't help but be nervous as I remembered the last couple of times I saw my father.

Six months before, he had been to see me in Los Angeles and he didn't have any fun. He spent most of the trip complaining about little things—things that didn't seem important at the time but really got him down. Perhaps he felt I was spending too much time with Julie and I wasn't paying him enough attention. I don't know. But I do know that it was very unusual for us to bicker like that. My whole life I'd wanted to be like my dad. He was just a nice person. He was a good man who was warm and compassionate and very easygoing. He'd always been so supportive of me—in my career, in my sexuality, in allowing me to be who I needed to be—that I was disturbed by this seeming change in him, this differentness that I had never seen before.

A few months after that, I went to a family wedding in Eureka Springs, Arkansas. My cousin Andrea was getting married. I flew into the Fayetteville airport and my dad picked me up. He was extremely irritable, much grumpier than usual, even more so than in L.A. a few months before. On the drive to the hotel, he began to talk about the L.A. trip—how he felt I wasn't his little Missy anymore, how Hollywood and everything had changed me. It was the first time my father had ever confronted me about anything that he didn't like about me. He was just so irritable and annoyed, and he kept touching his stomach like something was bothering him there.

All of this flashed quickly through my mind as I waited for my parents at the airport. And when my father walked off the plane, my worst expectations were realized. He looked like a different man. Like a man who was under a death sentence. A man who knew he was going to die. Which he was.

Through his sickness, during his last few months of life in Los Angeles, I began to understand that he had spent his entire life suppressing negative feelings and emotions. He grew up in a really tough environment. His father was an alcoholic, and I think that dad had a very damaging upbringing as a young boy. A big reason that I feel the need to try and be so truthful, to really communicate my feelings, is because I have this theory that maybe cancer is a result of keeping all of that emotion, especially anger, stuffed down inside. A lot of people disagree with me on this, but I really believe that part of illness directly correlates with how you deal with your emotions.

So much of that time with my father, after his diagnosis, was spent dealing with all those emotions, which were struggling to get out. I can't ever think of a time when my father got angry. Those last few months of his life, I think he was really trying to make up for all of those years of suppression, trying to purge all of that pent-up emotion out of his body—and out of his mind. He tried to get angry. He said some pretty angry things that helped me understand that those emotions were there all along—they had just never surfaced. He talked about his father—his father's alcoholism and abusive behavior; his life as the son of poverty-stricken migrant workers, and growing up with dreams that were never fulfilled.

He spoke about my mom, my sister, and me, too. I finally understood how hard it must have been for my father to have been so supportive of me and my career early on. He was driving me all over the state every weekend, leaving my mother at home alone. It had never occurred to me before that this might have been a hardship on their relationship. But it was. And my father let me know that. Which I'm grateful for. He allowed me to see a lot of things about my life, about my family's life, that I might otherwise never have known.

Still, in keeping with long family tradition, we never talked about his actual death. There was no discussion of what to do with his body, how he'd like to be buried, or cremated, or any of that. It was just the day-to-day conversation about this medicine, or that nurse. We talked around the issue as much as we possibly could. None of us wanted to admit that he was actually going to die.

I had to go away for a few days. When I got back to Los Angeles, my mother was worried—really worried. She told me that my dad seemed to be getting sicker and more delirious. When I went to see him, he kept talking about how Netty was coming. Netty was his sister, my aunt. "Netty's coming on Wednesday." We kept trying to tell him that Netty wasn't arriving until next week, but he insisted that she'd be there on Wednesday.

The morning that my father died, my entire family went to the hospital to be by his side. The doctors had informed me that there was really nothing else that could be done for my dad. Everybody had left the room except me, and I held his hand and looked into his eyes, and we talked and laughed. I am sure that because of the morphine running through his body, he wasn't in a lot of pain. We talked about fishing and ice cream. The doctor had come back

66048

*Dad has always been
my angel.*

```
Don't be afraid
Close your eyes
Lay it all down
Don't you cry
Can't you see we're going
Where we can see the sun rise
I've been talking to my angel
And He said that it's alright

I've always had to run
I don't know just why
Desire slowly smoking
Under the midwest sky
There's something waiting out there
Waiting for you and I
I've been talking to my angel
And He said that we should try

This town thinks I'm crazy
They just think I'm strange
Some folks want to own me
The rest just wish I'd change
But I can feel the thunder
Underneath my feet
I sold my soul for freedom
It's lonely but it's sweet

Don't be afraid
Close your eyes
Lay it all down
Don't you cry
Can't you see I'm going
Where I can see the sun rise
I've been talking to my angel
And he said that it's alright
```

*"Talking to My Angel"
was originally called
"66048," my
Leavenworth zip code.*

into the room to check on my dad, and he said that it was only a matter of time. The whole family had braced ourselves for a very long night of waiting for my father to die.

After the doctor left, for the last time, I looked into my father's big brown eyes, spoke quietly to him, and made him a final promise. I said, "You know, it's okay. You can go. I'll take care of everybody. I'll take care of Jennifer." And after giving that deathbed promise, I watched my father let go and die. For twenty minutes, his body became still and I could feel his spirit go away. His eyes were locked on mine until they became distant, fixed, and, finally, lifeless. I said to him again, "It's okay. You can go." And he did.

My dad died on Tuesday. His sister Netty came to town the next day. Wednesday. Just as he'd said.

That promise I made to my dad on his deathbed has been an internal battle ever since the words came out of my mouth. I have a lot of guilt about how I feel because, over the years, I have come to resent my sister so much for all of her attempts to manipulate me. I have generously provided for her and her children, and, though it kills me inside, I probably always will because of that promise I made to my father.

My relationship with my father was flawed, but I sure do wish that he were here today. There's so much we never got the chance to talk about. So many things that I think he would have been able to enjoy, like being a grandfather to my children. I know he is with me in spirit. I can feel him all around me. And I talk to him all of the time, as if he were right there next to me. I buried my dad in Los Angeles because I think that he wanted to stay near me.

Yes I Am

. . .

As soon as I could, I went back into the studio to finish *Never Enough*. I liked the album, but there was one particular song that didn't work. "Yes, I Am" was an offbeat song in three-four time, which just isn't very rock and roll. So I dropped the song from the album, figuring it was just one of those things that would stay in a drawer somewhere.

Things at home were great. Julie was so focused about her movie, *Teresa's Tattoo*, and was really driving herself and her career forward. It was still so attractive to me: the way she just made decisions about things, the way she just went for it. I went back on the road, but, professionally, things seemed to be in a slump. *Never Enough* wasn't selling very well—definitely not as well as the first two albums had—and there wasn't any hit on the radio to drive things forward. I was a little dismayed, but tried to put it behind me. I told myself, "Okay, that didn't work." So I just hunkered down to write more songs.

It was always so easy for me to write on the road. The rumble of the bus's engine, the towns flashing by the window. I'd sit in the back of the bus and think. It was just like being in my parents' basement as a child. A place where I felt safe. Safe to create. Safe to make something that I could be proud of. Something that spoke to who I really was.

K.d. lang's album, *Ingénue,* had been released the same day as *Never Enough,* in 1992. Just prior to the release of her album, k.d. publicly came out in an interview she gave to *The Advocate.* She kind of slipped out of the closet in that interview. "Constant Craving" was a hit, and it was kind of cool seeing how everyone accepted her announcing she was gay. We used to have conversations about it long before either one of us openly admitted our sexuality to the world. K.d. had gone through a period when she was getting tons of hate mail and threats because of an antimeat campaign she was a part of. She couldn't imagine what kind of response she'd get if she admitted to being gay. It was a real worry. We talked about it and made the commitment that someday we were going to do it. Someday, somehow. We'd fantasize about coming out and talking about it. Then, one day, she did it. It was great. Nothing bad happened, and that was so cool to see. Her album did really well and there was no fallout, which was totally inspiring.

At the end of 1992, Julie became very politically involved with Bill Clinton and the presidential election. As it went along, I did a couple of benefits and we participated in a Young Democrats fundraiser at the Santa Monica airport. Bill and Hillary were attending, but they were late so the organizers kept telling me to stall. I played song after song until they got there. Bill spoke to the crowd and, before he left later that night, he came over to say hello to me. He took one look at Julie and he started checking her out. He didn't know she was with me. All he saw was an attractive, dark-haired girl, and he just zoomed her. She was like *woo!* He was very charming, that former president.

Thankfully, he was elected and Julie and I got invited to the inauguration. The first day of that whole inaugural weekend, I participated in a concert that Quincy Jones was putting together. It was a really big deal and quite an honor to be involved in—on any level. We were performing on the steps of the Lincoln Memorial, and it was everyone from Aretha Franklin to Michael Jackson, Michael Stipe from REM, and Diana Ross. I sang a duet with Jon Secada. President and Mrs. Clinton and Vice President and Mrs. Gore were sitting right in front of us. It was really overwhelming.

The next day was the inauguration. Seeing a man sworn in as the president of the United States is a very emotional experience. There was a woman sitting one row in front of us crying, and I asked her what was wrong. She explained that she had never been to a swearing-in ceremony before, but that she had been to the White House as a protester. This was the first time she had been invited as a guest. She was overwhelmed by the power and feeling of positive change that was in the air that day, and it brought her to tears.

That night, the Human Rights Campaign, the National Gay and Lesbian Task Force, and other gay organizations were having the Triangle Ball. They had donated a lot of money to Clinton's campaign to help get him elected. They rallied the gay and lesbian voters to vote for him. It was the first time gays and lesbians were invited to the ceremony. Julie and I went to that ball. It was at the Washington Press Club, and there were just people everywhere. There was a balcony above the crowd and we decided to go up there with k.d. lang and Cassandra Peterson, a.k.a. Elvira. Cassandra was talking to the crowd, and she introduced k.d. There were monitors all over the room showing us up on that balcony. It was so strange. K.d. told the crowd that coming out was the best thing she ever did. And then she introduced me to the crowd. I don't know why I did it—it certainly wasn't my plan—but I came out. I walked up to the microphone and said, "Hi. I'm real proud to say I'm a lesbian." The crowd went crazy. K.d. gave me this huge hug. It really startled everyone, including me. I thought maybe I'd go on Arsenio Hall's show and go public, but it didn't happen that way. I walked away from the microphone and Julie said to me, "I think you came out." I went and sat down in the hall. And she sat with me and we just sat there and went "Well, okay. I'm out." Both of us were kind of stunned.

Julie laughed and said, "I guess you should make some phone calls tomorrow." By the time I had made them, my publicist already knew. It was in all of the morning papers. It wasn't a revelation, but it wasn't expected.

I think *The Washington Post* ran a story about all of the different inaugural balls, and when it came to the Gay and Lesbian Triangle Ball, I was referenced as butch rocker Melissa Etheridge. All of a sudden I'm a butch rocker. Now that I've come out as a lesbian, I'm butch according to the newspaper.

Soon after that, I went back into the studio to make my new album. It was actually quite a traumatic experience. After the underwhelming sales of *Never Enough*, my record company insisted I get a new producer. I chose Hugh Padgam, who'd had great success with the Police, Sting, and XTC. This forced me into the position of telling Kevin that his days of producing with me were over. Although Hugh did a great job, I felt bad about Kevin. Even more so when the album was partially recorded and the record company again came back to me and said they thought the bass was "weak." So I had to re-record a number of Kevin's bass tracks for the album.

At that point, Kevin felt completely cut off from the process and decided that he couldn't play with me anymore. Fritz was his friend, so he felt the need to follow Kevin out of the band.

There I was, finishing a new album, about to tour, and I didn't have a band. Luckily, I ran into an old friend, John Shanks, at a benefit. John's a brilliant guitarist; I'd worked with him years earlier. Our collaboration didn't work out then, but he had clearly changed. He'd made some choices in his life and was much more open to the idea of working wholeheartedly with me. When I offered him the opportunity to tour with me, he loved the idea. He helped me find my drummer, Kenny Aronoff, and my bassist, Mark Browne, and all three of them play with me to this day.

After I'd recorded all the songs for the new album, I thought back to the one that had been dropped from *Never Enough*. "Yes, I Am." Having just come out, I re-recorded the song and thought, "Well, why don't we just name the album *Yes I Am*, even though the song is not about my coming out or being gay. It's a song about how I was feeling toward Julie. The words are really strong and declarative. "Am I your passion, your promise, your end? Yes I am." It was just about my commitment to Julie—about our love, about my relationship. Am I possessive and obsessive and all these things I talk about in that song? I say I am.

After outing myself so publicly, I wanted the title of the album to be a positive, self-affirming statement. *Yes I Am*. Owning it. Yes, this is what I am. Yes, I am. That's how I was feeling. I was finally feeling, yes, *this* is what I am. Even the photos for the *Yes I Am* album were reflective of who I am and of me being more like me. Some of the photos on *Never Enough* were an attempt to look more glamorous, which was so far away from how I naturally feel good about myself. I like being in jeans and T-shirts and I don't wear a lot of makeup. *Yes I Am* was my return to the core of who I am. It felt real. It felt very whole. This is who I am, and the songs on that album are really strong pieces of me.

Once I had come out, k.d. and I bugged the crap out of Ellen DeGeneres. We were always trying to get her to come out. For me, it had only been a matter of time before I was outed by a magazine or some other publication. The last article I did before publicly declaring that I am gay was in a magazine called *Music Express*. The article intimated my sexuality, and I had gotten fed up with hiding it.

When I released *Yes I Am*, I had to do interviews in every town I played in, which meant that the local newspaper, the college newspaper, television interviewers, and radio interviewers all wanted me to talk about coming out and being queer. I talked about it ten times a day, which was strange at first because I had *never* talked about it before. I guess it was a new thing after all these years of just kind of speaking ambiguously about everything.

Audiences just went insane after hearing the news that I was a lesbian. It certainly brought more gays out to my concerts. I had a large lesbian following anyway, but once I came out, all of a sudden, the crowds grew and grew and it was insanely wonderful. But I was thrust into a new position—becoming almost a "poster child" for gay and lesbian causes and issues. I never felt like a spokeswoman before coming out. I was just telling a good story through my music. Now I feel like a spokeswoman for gays and lesbians, gay families, and gay divorce. In fact, I think I am better known for who I am as a gay woman than as a musician. That has taken a little getting used to over the years.

The other side of success was that I was out of town constantly. Julie and I had less and less time together. I just toured and toured, the venues getting larger, the crowds getting bigger. There's such a myth about being on the road. You know, bands

Joy Widmark doing my makeup before a show in Sacramento

Steven Girmant,
my tour manager,
is always there for me.

Sound check in San Francisco © 1996 Melissa Etheridge/Photo by Nicole Bengiveno / Matrix

With Bill Leopold, my manager, before a show © 1996 Melissa Etheridge/Photo by Nicole Bengiveno / Matrix

trashing hotel rooms, sleeping with groupies. Party until you have to do the show. That was never my road. Mine looked a lot like going to work. And, like anyone at work, I thought about home a lot. Julie and I would talk every night. But, after such a long time on buses and planes with other people, home life seems so distant. And you expect that other person to be the same person you left behind. But that person is growing and changing just like you are. And it's easy to forget that.

Being on the road this time created a distance between Julie and me. I couldn't understand the things she was trying to convey to me from halfway around the world. I couldn't figure out what it was she wanted from me. I begged her to wait for me to come home so we could deal with things.

It was exactly that sort of miscommunication between us that had caused me to write "Come to My Window." It's got to be the most misunderstood song I've written. It was one of my biggest hits, but it's not the love song everyone perceives it to be. This song was so huge that there's even a Muzak version. "Come to My Window" stayed on the Billboard Top 40 chart longer than any other record at the time.

People seem to think that "Come to My Window" is this tender love song, "Come to my window, crawl inside and wait by the light of the moon. Come to my window. I'll be home soon." I still don't know why it was such a big hit. I just don't get it because this is a very veiled song. It's all about the troubles I was having at home. Julie and I were beginning to have such a hard time.

When I was on that tour, I would just call Julie up from wherever I was, and, since it seemed like every conversation would turn into a fight, I would dial the phone long distance and just sit there and listen to her breathe on the other end of the line. I would have done anything not to fight, even if it meant listening to her silence.

Just to reach her and know that she was on the phone gave me hope. I was trying to just get from her an "I love you," an acceptance. She so represented my mother to me—that same distant and aloof attitude. I could close my eyes and see both of them, my mother closing the door to her bedroom, shutting me out with a book in her hand, and Julie, sitting in our home, reading in the chair in our bedroom. I just felt so left out, so lost and confused.

Metaphorically, I felt as if I couldn't even walk through our front door at home. Every phone call was a fight. We were not seeing eye-to-eye on anything. We weren't coming together on anything. We couldn't agree to meet at the front door, so you know what? Come to my window, just meet me on the other side of the house, you know, and wait, because I'll be home soon. I was on the road, touring, but it was toward the end of my tour and I kept reminding Julie to hang in there. I'd be coming home soon, and we would work everything out between us. It's a harshly truthful song that got misconstrued as a love song. I think Julie had a hard time with it because, to her, it was me saying, "Oh, come on, can't we just compromise? Can't you meet me somewhere else, other than what you are thinking?" From what I could see, Julie took the song very personally, hearing that she was supposed to just sit around and wait for me. Maybe she thought that I was trying to say to her, "I know you're trying to get me to see something. Wait for me. I'll get there soon." I don't think she ever liked it.

COME TO MY WINDOW

Come to my window
Crawl inside, wait by the light of the moon
Come to my window
I'll be home soon

I would dial the numbers
Just to listen to your breath
I would stand inside my hell
And hold the hand of death
You don't know how far I'd go
To ease this precious ache
You don't know how much I'd give
Or how much I can take
Just to reach you
Just to reach you
Oh to reach you

Keeping my eyes open
I cannot afford to sleep
Giving away promises
I know that I can't keep
Nothing fills the blackness
That has seeped into my chest
I need you in my blood
I am forsaking all the rest
Just to reach you
Just to reach you
Oh to reach you

I don't care what they think
I don't care what they say
What do they know about this love anyway?

The response to *Yes I Am* was incredible. I wasn't playing theaters anymore, I was headlining arenas now. What a rush it was. Finally, I had made it. Made it by being exactly who I am and what I am. A lesbian rock and roller.

The first time I felt like "Oh, maybe I'm making a difference in the gay and lesbian community" was when I played at Woodstock in the summer of 1994. I was supposed to go on stage right after Henry Rollins and before Nine Inch Nails. There were people as far as I could see. It had just rained during Rollins's set and the whole field was turning into mud. During my set, the sun came out but I could see a patch of people getting muddier and muddier. During my last song, "Like the Way I Do," I broke the song down to a tribal-rhythm guitar solo. This whole sea of muddy people started to make their way toward the stage like a big muddy tribe. Their exuberance was infectious; it fed me and I fed them. Just as their dancing broke into a wild frenzy I looked up and saw this one big old rainbow flag waving in the crowd. It was just a huge "Wow!" Something I will never forget. To be up there singing at Woodstock—which always represented our nation's youth culture, and the fight against the war, and all kinds of protest stuff—and to see gay men and women waving their flag, and nobody beating them up. Nothing bad happened and it was incredible to feel so connected and so full of hope and peace.

One of the glorious things about suddenly being as famous as I was then is that people call you up on the phone and ask you to do really cool things. I got a phone call from MTV. They wanted to do an *Unplugged* with me. I spoke to one of their producers, and I told him that I wanted to do the show solo because that was where I came from in my career. Just me, unplugged. They agreed, but the producer asked me if there was anybody I wanted to sing with. I hadn't really thought about that, but my lifelong dream was to sing with Bruce Springsteen, ha-ha. I tell the producer this, half joking, thinking there's no way *that'll* happen, and he says, "All right. Well, we'll see what we can do."

Bruce was a HUGE influence on me. The way he wove his life into his music. The way he told his stories. The way he just got up on stage and *did* it. No opening act, as few barriers as possible between him and his audience. I had always thought of him as one of

*My good friends
Meg Ryan and
Laura Dern visited
the studio while I
was making* Skin.

*Jamming to "Pink
Cadillac" with
Bruce Springsteen
at my show in
Milwaukee, 1996*

Julie, Jann Wenner, John Sykes, and me at the Rock and Roll Hall of Fame induction dinner in New York City, 2000

Dermott Mulroney played cello (left) on "Place Your Hand" while (above) k. d. lang and I played for fun at home.

my heroes, one of those people who had gone before me and had done it right.

The next day, MTV called me back and told me that Bruce said he'd do the show. The next day! I was going to do his song "Thunder Road" anyway. I was planning to pay tribute to my musical influences, like Bruce, and Janis Joplin. I could have done anything with him. I just kept thinking, "No, he's not going to do that. Someone's telling me a lie. Someone's making this up."

But, sure enough, when I got to the MTV studio, there he was. He came backstage during the sound check, and we sat down to rehearse—just Bruce and me playing. I was just out of my mind, I was crazy nervous.

We worked out who sings what, who sings harmonies, and so on. For some reason, I wanted to sing the line "So Mary, climb in" and then we'd both sing the last two lines together: "It's a town full of losers and we're pulling out of here to win."

Throughout that show, all I could think about was singing with Bruce. I kept thinking, "Five more songs until Bruce comes out. Four more songs until Bruce comes out." I was just counting down the songs. I was so up, and the audience didn't even know he was there.

I started talking to the audience about my influences, and I went into this whole story about Bruce Springsteen. I told the audience that the producers of *Unplugged* had asked me who I wanted to sing with and I said Bruce and then I said, "You know what?" He said "Yes." And I started to play the opening of "Thunder Road." It was just the most amazing thing. Up to then, I had done every song perfectly. I played great and it was very professional. But I start in singing with him, and we got to the line where I'm supposed to sing, "So, Mary, climb in." And I'm, like, five feet away from the microphone, just looking at him.

He turned around and looked at me, because I had totally flubbed the line. So at the end of the song, the director wants to do another take, which was fine with me. I got to play with Bruce again. We did a second take, and once again, I'm standing there just looking at him. He cracked up. I managed to get the line out and we finished the song. Bruce Springsteen singing with me that night is burned deep in my memory. He gave me a big kiss. It was crazy and sooo fun. It was one of the top moments in my performing life, ever.

After I made *Yes I Am*, Julie and I felt that we had outgrown our Hollywood house, and we started looking for a larger home. I'm not certain of the significance, but Julie and I had a tendency to move a lot during our relationship. We finally found this great old Spanish-style home in the Outpost area of L.A. It was a wonderful old gorgeous house with lots of character. While I went on tour to promote the album, Julie stayed at home and fixed up that house for us.

I thought that things were really starting to get back into a good groove between us, but Julie met a man whom she became very attracted to. In the beginning, she was just having lunches with him and discussing business. He was in the entertainment business, and Julie had an interest in directing films, so it didn't seem too unusual for them to be hanging out. I never worried that anything was going on between them. I thought it was business and so I supported the friendship. He wasn't a threat to me. At least I never thought he was.

Julie told me that she had been spending some time with him and that she was starting to develop a strong attraction. At the time, I didn't think there was a real possibility that the two of them would connect—certainly not on a physical level. Maybe I was denying the possibility to justify my own feelings, but I just didn't think about it at the time. At this point, there was so much uncertainty in our relationship, and this added a whole new level—one I wasn't psychologically prepared for.

One day, Julie came home from one of her lunch meetings and proceeded to inform me that she had kissed this guy. In the same way that she explained her attraction to k.d. years earlier, she started to tell me that she missed men in her life and she thought that she might want to sleep with this guy. I just stopped cold in my tracks. No way! I was not going to go through this cycle again. It was not okay with me. I think I might have surprised her with my absolute refusal to accept what she was telling me. I think that she thought it was going to be fine, that it had been a while since the k.d. thing, and that I would surely understand her needs. Boy, was she wrong!

Once again, I felt as if I had no choice in the matter. If I forbade Julie, I truly believed that she would leave me. I just couldn't bear that thought of her sleeping with someone else. But even worse was the thought of not having Julie in my life. That scared me even more. Julie and I had a way of making everything okay in our relationship by connecting sexually. It didn't matter what had transpired in the past. All she had to do was touch me, love me, make love to me, and it was all forgiven. The slate would be wiped clean. It was like a great big Band-Aid. At the time, I didn't have the strength to stand my ground about this. I was too insecure to say to her, "Stop. Don't do this. It's not okay." I didn't have the sense of myself—that I would rather be alone than be with a lover who needed to be with other people.

I chose to believe that her attraction to men was about the physical connection that I felt I could never give to Julie. For the most part, we had a great relationship, but at the end of the day, even though we were very, very sexual, there was that one thing that I could never offer to Julie that she was now telling me she needed.

This went on for months. And for the first time in my rela-tionship experience, this was something that I could do nothing about in terms of satisfying her need. I got to the point where I wasn't going to beat my head against the wall over it anymore. I was in Montreal doing a show, and I came to the realization that Julie was still seeing this man, and it became very clear that she was going to do whatever she wanted anyway. So, I finally told her to go and do whatever it was that she wanted. It wasn't good.

Five years later, she admitted to me that she had slept with this man. I asked her why she never told me, and she said that I never asked. All I could say was, "Fuck you!" Montreal was the be-ginning of the end for us. Though I did my best to ignore it, our re-lationship was a slippery slope from that point on.

Your Little Secret

...

ON THE SURFACE, THOUGH, EVERYTHING WAS FINE WITH Julie and me. While we struggled to discuss and diffuse our issues, biology began to rear its ugly head. After we moved in together, we would fantasize about having children, but "eventually" was always the key word. We had acquired our family pets: two dogs and two cats. The cats came first. Julie is more of a "cat person" than I am. And then we got our first dog, Angel.

Julie and I were in Sacramento, California, for a show. When I'm on tour, a list gets posted backstage for items that anyone might need a runner to go out and get. We get very little free time on the road, so there is a person who is available to get toothpaste, deodorant—whatever. I was being smart-alecky one day, and I decided to write "One small warm puppy" on the runner's list. Later that day, my tour manager walked in with this tiny, cute, sweet-faced puppy. We played with her for about an hour, and my tour manager said that he had to take her back to the pet store. She was only on loan. Right before I went on stage, Julie said to me, "I feel like I just gave away my best friend." While I was on stage, she went to the pet store, and, the next day, we took Angel home with us. Bingo came along a few years later, just before Julie got pregnant for the first time. Bingo was a street dog that a friend of ours had rescued and brought to our house. Angel and Bingo played around in the yard and they loved each other, so we adopted Bingo. Being "mommies" to our animals was enough for us—for a while, anyway.

I wasn't sure that I really wanted to have kids at first. I didn't know what it would be like, and I think I was afraid of the impact it would have on my life. I didn't have any concept of what becoming a parent would mean. It is a life-changing miracle, but I didn't know that then. I went along with the fantasy at first, even though a part of me disagreed with the idea. I had always felt that maybe I was too professionally and personally self-centered to have children. I couldn't imagine taking nine months off to be pregnant, and not being able to work. I just couldn't imagine myself doing it. I wouldn't have pushed for it, but I would never have denied my partner the opportunity to be a parent either. But the idea of sharing that kind of bond was intriguing to me too, because, like a lot of couples, I thought having a kid might help our relationship.

After I released *Yes I Am*, our standard of living radically improved, and I sensed that, no matter what, I would be financially sound for the rest of my life. Julie and I had settled into our life together. We had been together four years, and she started talking about and exploring the idea of having children. She was in her early thirties and was beginning to have strong maternal feelings. I had gotten to a place in my career where, if I chose to take a year off, I could do so at any time. Financially and careerwise, I had reached a peak. I had done it. I had achieved everything I set out to do.

When Julie came to me and said that she was seriously ready to have a baby, we talked about this need of hers to still be with men sexually. She reassured me that she wanted to have a family with me, and *that* desire was stronger than her longing to be with a man. I believed her. I persuaded myself that if she wanted to have children with me, then she must want me forever. That's how I made things right in my head. Children are a pretty serious commitment. Children meant forever, in my mind. There was never a thought that there could be any other way.

I had definitely sowed my oats. I was living with this fantastic woman with whom I wanted to spend the rest of my life. For so many years, I had defined who I was by my partner. And my partner wanted kids. Our fantasy was quickly becoming a viable reality. It had entered the realm of the possible. We hadn't planned it out yet, but it was there. It was closer. I could tell that we would definitely have children soon.

In early 1994, Julie and I took our first trip to Hawaii. We stayed in a lovely hotel across the bay from Graham Nash's house. Graham had given us the name of a real estate agent to call because Julie and I were thinking of renting a house the next time we vacationed in Hawaii. When we spoke to the agent, she informed us that David and Jan Crosby were staying at Graham's house and gave us the number to call.

There is a running debate, between David Crosby and me, about whether I first met him while I was playing in Toledo, Ohio, or at a benefit concert for Voters For Choice, in Washington, D.C. He says it was in Toledo while he was performing with Stills and Nash. I was on the road, and I got a call that it was David's birthday. Would I come over and sing "Happy Birthday" to him, on stage, during his show? Of course, I said yes. David thinks that's the first time we met. But I think I had met him earlier, at the Voters For Choice benefit. It's so bizarre that neither of us is sure which meeting was our first. The truth is, we can't remember. I do recall walking out on stage and singing "Happy Birthday" to him in Toledo. He was really surprised. And it's funny because he'll laugh and say to me, "I didn't know anything about you. And I kind of had a fancy for you." Turns out that he ended up being the father of my children, so there.

Anyway, I contend that the first time we met was at the Voters For Choice benefit, and since this is my book, I'm sticking with that story. Julie and I were in the van with him, driving from the hotel to the concert. David is a wonderful, personable man who has a larger-than-life personality. He's completely fun-loving. We had gotten caught in traffic, and in order for us to be on time for the show, we had to get out and walk to the concert with everybody else. It was quite unexpected for everybody to see David Crosby and Melissa Etheridge just walking through the entrance gate. We had a lot of fun with it. We said "Hello" and thanked everyone we met for coming to the show. It turned out to be a bonding night for us, and we became fast friends after that.

Not long after that benefit, David's wife, Jan, got pregnant. Around that same time, David was told that he needed a liver transplant. And as if that wasn't enough stuff to deal with at one time, right after Jan had her baby, David discovered that he had a thirty-six-year-old son he knew nothing about. It was an insane year for David and Jan. We'd see them socially as often as we could, but it wasn't as often as we would have liked. Julie and I thought the world of David and Jan. They are two incredible human beings who have been through a lot.

We wanted to go over to visit them because David was still recuperating from his surgery, and Django, their son, was barely six months old. We had a great time visiting with them during that week, and having just had a baby themselves, the topic of kids came up. We confided to them that we were seriously thinking about having children.

Until that point, Julie and I had had some deep discussions about *how* we would get pregnant and what our parenting philosophies consisted of. I couldn't imagine getting pregnant at that point in my career, but the ticking of Julie's biological clock was getting louder by the month. She was ready to do it. For a lot of different reasons, we decided that she would be the one to carry the baby. She wanted to do it. She wanted to have that experience. We also decided that artificial insemination was, for us, the best method for getting pregnant. I was still having some major issues with Julie's desire to be with a man, and the thought of her making love with the father of our baby was too much for me to handle. It would have been a wedge between us, and, I also believe, between the child and me. If Julie had insisted on having intercourse with a man to get pregnant, then because of our past and as difficult as it would have been for me, I resigned myself to accepting that method, as long as I could be there at the conception. It was important to me because it was something that I would never be able to give to her myself. I wanted to be as involved as possible. We had also discussed the idea of harvesting my eggs, fertilizing them, and then having Julie carry the embryo through the miracle of in-vitro fertilization. The surgery to harvest the eggs is a major operation, and the recovery time for me would have been fairly significant. I also had fibroid tumors in my uterus, which made my periods very painful, and they were getting worse and worse. My doctor told me that I would probably have a difficult time getting pregnant. In the scheme of things, I knew that it didn't matter to me one bit where our children came from, Julie's body or mine. They would always be *our* children. The blood connection didn't make a difference to me at all.

We talked about using a sperm bank, but we felt it was important that our children know who their biological father is and understand their lineage and the people they have come from. Their father would not have to be in their life all the time, but when they asked whether they have a daddy, we wanted to be able to say to them, "Yes, and this is who he is."

David and Jan started asking us if we had considered anyone to be the donor, and we told them that we had. Aside from Brad Pitt, who was mentioned in a tabloid rumor, we were considering any number of people from Jackson Browne to an old high-school friend of Julie's to my tour manager, Steven Girmant. We never had a conversation about this with any of these men, so none of them even knew he was on our list. We were just musing about possible donors. People have asked me whether a musical background was an essential factor in our decision. The truth is, it wasn't ever really a factor. I don't believe that there is such a thing as an inherited music gene. Other than myself, there's no musical talent to speak of in my family, so I never gave it much thought in making this decision. Looks didn't play a big part in our decision, either. It wasn't like we were trying to find someone who had features similar to my own so that the kids would truly resemble both of us. It was really a special situation and only a very special person would understand that being a biological parent did not obligate him or include him in parenting the child in any way, beyond the biological gift. We wanted someone who could understand and accept that he is the child's biological father, but no parenting is involved. That's not an easy situation for anyone. It is a difficult line. Some men would be fine with it, in theory; others would simply not be able to separate the two roles.

As we continued our talk with David and Jan that day, Jan said to us, "Well, what about David?" Julie and I just looked at each other—none of us had given any thought to this before. David stood there for a moment, contemplating the idea, and then said, "Yeah, what about me?" We couldn't believe that he was being serious. They had just had a child themselves, and they knew the glorious miracle of childbirth—the blessing of it. And David's life had just been saved. He had a whole newfound love of life, because someone had just given him a new liver. Now he could give us something so that we might have a life as parents. It was very beautiful. The gesture was selfless and pure. When we left the house that day, we reminded ourselves that they had made the generous offer rather quickly and offhandedly. Maybe they didn't realize what they were offering. Julie kept asking me whether I thought they were serious. I just kept saying, "Well, I don't know."

We talked about it for a year or so before we made the decision. It was such an incredible offer. We had some concerns about David's past health issues. We considered his earlier addiction problems, but we knew that he was fully recovered and had been sober for eight years. Julie researched everything we needed to know about sperm. She found out that sperm regenerates itself every seventy-two hours, so anything he had done in the past would not be an issue for this pregnancy. We knew that addiction can be inherited, and because Julie and I both have family histories of addiction, transmission of an addiction gene would have been possible anyway. We were willing to take that chance. David and Jan had a new baby who was in perfect health. We knew this couple, we respected and loved them, and they were not a part of our everyday life. We decided that we would call them and see if they were serious. Turns out, they were.

Pregnancy

...

BEING THE PERFECT VIRGO, JULIE STARTED THE PROCESS of preparing her body for pregnancy with precision and perfection. She started marking charts of her ovulation cycles. She knew exactly what day she could get pregnant. Then she factored in my touring schedule. By this time, my next album, *Your Little Secret*, had come out, and I was getting ready to go on an eight-month tour of America and Europe. We backdated nine months from the end of my tour (January 1997) and we figured that the first date Julie could get pregnant would be in May 1996. After my eight months of touring, I'd be home and available to take some time off in January.

We decided that we would try to get pregnant in May. Julie had it all worked it out, right down to the day. She made the call to the Crosbys. It just so happened that David was to be in L.A. on the exact day that Julie was ovulating. He was rehearsing with Stills and Nash for a show. He said that he'd come by the house that afternoon and drop "it" by. I remember that we had painters working on the house, and we wondered what they would think when

David Crosby stopped by the house to deliver a curious-looking brown paper bag.

We lit some candles in the bedroom, and we were nervous waiting for David to bring the stuff. David drove up in a big black Suburban. Sure enough, the painters were having lunch outside, and they saw David Crosby get out with this brown paper bag. I answered the door, he handed it to me, and gave me a big hug and a kiss. All I could say was, "Thank you so much." I was really moved. He got back in the Suburban and drove off.

Julie had been to the fertility doctor before the day of conception, so she was fully aware of the procedure. Our doctor was the same doctor Jan and David had used for the birth of their son, so he knew that David's sperm was good. Julie had asked the doctor if the procedure had to take place in his office or if we could do it ourselves at home. The doctor reassured us that as long as we got the sperm in the right place, we could easily get pregnant at home. David had delivered the gift in a plastic prescription cup that had a lid on it. We had the little baby-size medicine syringe. We made love. We took that gift and placed it where it needed to be, and we waited. We stayed in bed for a little while, and I asked Julie, "Well, are you pregnant?" Of course, we wouldn't know for two weeks, but Julie was convinced that she could feel it happening inside her later that day. She kept saying, "I know it's happening. I can feel it right here." She insisted that she felt herself getting pregnant.

She obviously knows her body. I thought we'd be doing this for months. I couldn't believe that it could be so easy. Every day for the next two weeks, Julie kept checking to see whether she was pregnant. She went to the doctor, who reaffirmed that it was too soon to know. She peed on a stick. She had a blood test. She was just so anxious to know. After about ten days, she was getting frustrated. Two weeks after we had made love, Julie got out of bed really early. I think it was around six in the morning. I remember lying in bed and hearing the rustling of paper, and something opening. I thought, "Damn, she's started her period." I turned around and I went back to sleep. The next thing I heard was Julie saying, "Melissa, come in here. Can you read this? Tell me what it says." It was like that television commercial where the couples find out whether they are pregnant! I was like Dick Van Dyke. I fell out of the bed and went to the bathroom.

"Is that two lines?"

"Yes," I said, "that is definitely two lines." She got dressed, went to the doctor, and got a blood test to be sure. She called me later and said, "Yes, I'm pregnant." It doesn't always happen like that. We have known couples who tried for months, and even years. If you're lucky, it takes. Julie always said she had fertility guilt. Boom! First try. We called David and Jan and gave them the news. They were thrilled for us.

It's such a journey when you're pregnant. The first twelve weeks of pregnancy are the riskiest in terms of miscarriage. We didn't tell anybody that we were pregnant until after the first trimester. We didn't tell our parents. We didn't tell anybody. I think Julie told her closest, closest friend, but, for the most part, we were definitely lying low. Toward the end of the summer, word of Julie's pregnancy had leaked. I was about to begin touring in Europe with Bryan Adams, and Julie was four months pregnant, with raging hormones. Just before I left, we were faced with a sudden barrage of questions from the media.

The gist of the media position was: "Whoa, two lesbians; well, that's okay. But you're going to have a baby?" Everyone wanted to know how we did that. It certainly wasn't immaculate. It was a really intimate thing between the two of us, and we weren't ready to talk about how it happened. There were the big jokes that just seemed to go on and on and on. We've always had a very good sense of humor about everything. Even though we weren't looking to get any publicity out of Julie's pregnancy, there seemed to be a lot of questions, so we thought that we would agree to do one television interview and one print interview so that there would be no misconceptions about the birth of our child. We figured that if we gave these two interviews, everyone would leave us alone, and Julie could have a peaceful pregnancy and birth. We did *20/20* and *Newsweek*. We turned out to be the cover story of *Newsweek*.

I went to Europe and I basically toured the whole time Julie was pregnant. I think that was the biggest mistake I made. A pregnancy is an incredibly emotional, crazy time. Julie had never been pregnant before, and I think she felt I had left her all alone. It wasn't my intent; we had planned for me to be gone. But I was wracked with guilt over it. Being apart was very, very hard for both of us. We hadn't realized the impact being pregnant would have on our lives, on our relationship, and on each other. That I worked while Julie was pregnant is probably the only regret I have from that time. I tried to compensate by not working during her second pregnancy or for a year after our son Beckett was born.

As hard as it was, emotionally and physically, it was a pretty great pregnancy for Julie. She's so damn healthy, and so strong. Julie made it a point to stop smoking, even before she became pregnant. Quitting wasn't easy for her because she had been a smoker for a very long time. She ate all the right foods. She read every book ever written on pregnancy, childbirth, and parenting. We took a parenting class. She went to pregnancy yoga classes where she met our dear friends Alex and Heather. Heather's due date was the same as ours, and they were going to use the same midwife we had chosen to use for our birth.

I came off the road around Christmas. Julie was due January twenty-fifth. All of January, we just hung around the house waiting

I just want to go home.

© 1996 Melissa Etheridge/
Photo by Nicole Bengiveno / Matrix

*A quiet moment backstage with
Julie, during her pregnancy*

© 1996 Melissa Etheridge/
Photo by Nicole Bengiveno/Matrix

for the arrival of our baby. I watched a lot of football and did a lot of puzzles. Julie was certain that she was going to deliver two weeks early, so around January fourteenth, we were saying, "Any day now." January twenty-first rolled around and we were still saying, "Any day now." It started wearing on our last nerve. Then Julie's due date passed and the days kept going by. Day after day. I remember that every morning, Julie would cry. She would wake up and she'd still be pregnant. Those last few weeks were tough. She'd walk down the steps, trying to induce labor. She couldn't go anywhere or do anything. She was so pregnant and so over being pregnant. Those last four weeks were the slowest time that ever passed for me.

For most of the pregnancy, we had been calling the baby Austin. I had all sorts of little songs and rhymes made up about baby Austin. A few weeks before the baby was born, Julie said that she didn't think the baby felt like an Austin anymore, so we decided to go with Bailey, which was one of our other top choices. That's what happens when a baby is late. You have all of this time on your hands and you start to change your mind about everything.

Our good friend Laura Dern has her birthday on February tenth. On February second, she said to Julie, "Wouldn't it be funny if the baby was born on my birthday?" No, it wouldn't be funny at all. That would mean that Julie would be two weeks late, and we thought, "No way. It's not possible." But it was possible.

At 11:00 P.M. on the evening of February eighth, we had just turned out the lights to go to bed and I swear that I heard Julie's water break. It was like a small-sounding pop. One of the first rules of labor is to go back to sleep, but this was our first child and we were excited and not going back to sleep. By the next morning, she was in steady labor. The midwife came and said that she was dilated only a few centimeters and still had a long way to go. The baby was posterior. It hadn't turned yet in the uterus to come down

Bailey's groovy birth
announcement, drawn
by my bass player,
Mark Browne

Bailey

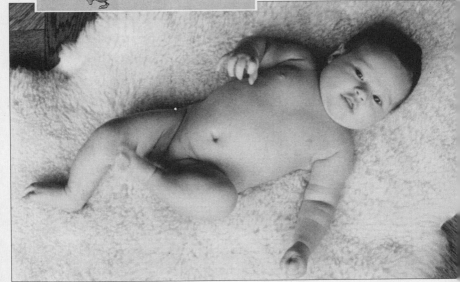

Reading about childbirth

Bailey and me

the birth canal headfirst. Julie was in back labor, which makes every contraction terribly painful. After twenty-four hours of labor and excruciating pain, Julie decided that it was time to go to a hospital. She was in a tremendous amount of pain.

I knew that there was a possibility that if Melissa Etheridge and Julie Cypher checked into a hospital to have their baby, there'd be an onslaught of media waiting for us pretty quickly thereafter. I just couldn't deal with that concept while Julie was in labor. So, I called Steven Girmant, my tour manager, and told him that we were heading to Cedars Sinai to have the baby. I knew that he could deal with all of the hurdles so that we could have Bailey in peace. I'm not sure how Steven beat us to the hospital that day. He lives in Manhattan Beach, about thirty minutes from the hospital, and we were coming from Beverly Hills, which is about five minutes away, but somehow he was there waiting for us when we arrived. He made sure that everything on a personal level was going to be taken care of. I swear, if a nurse had walked in and asked for an autograph, I would have lost it. But Steven was right there, keeping everyone calm, including myself. There's a certain comfort level that he gives my professional and my personal life.

We arrived at the hospital and Julie was given a light epidural. Within twenty minutes, she was completely dilated and ready to push. I was holding Julie's head, looking into a mirror where I could witness Bailey being born. It was miraculous. Words can't even begin to express how I felt as I saw my daughter being born. As I held her for the first time . . .

Despite our wish to not spend the night in the hospital, it was hospital policy that a pediatrician must check a newborn baby before it can be released. There was no pediatrician on call until early the next morning. So Julie and I hunkered down with our newborn in a small hospital bed until the morning.

Mothering

...

MY LIFE CHANGED FROM THE MOMENT I BECAME A PARENT. My role was no longer just as a partner or a gay rights activist or a rock-and-roll singer. I became half of the team that was now responsible for shaping and guiding the life of this beautiful child through the world. There's a certain sense of wonderfulness when you have that opportunity in front of you

I have to admit, though, it didn't happen instantaneously. I had thought that the moment I held my daughter everything would change and I would instantly understand motherhood. Of course it wasn't that easy. I held my daughter and I panicked. "Where's the instruction book?" I thought to myself. The world is actually trusting *me* with this newborn life? Honestly, I think I was more scared those first few days than anything else.

Our whole life became about our daughter. We would sleep with her. Breathe with her. Watch her tiny mouth as it strained for the nipple. Wipe her tiny butt when she pooped. Those first few months, the three of us were in a sort of familial bliss. Everything was about the baby.

Gradually, those feelings of fear and insecurity began to shift. I began to understand that raising a child is as much about raising myself. As a child, I learned that the only proper way to deal with intense emotion was to walk away. To ignore it. But I couldn't walk away from Bailey. I didn't want to ignore it. I wanted to steep myself in her presence. To really deal with what was going on inside this little life. It was scary. But it was also wonderful. In some sense, having Bailey forced me to grow up. To really deal with those issues that were still left over from my own childhood. I wanted her childhood to be different. To be full of the wonder and joy of life. I didn't want her to be scared or confused or need to build all those walls around herself that I had been building and breaking down all my life. I wanted her to be whole. And to model that for her, I had to find the wholeness within myself.

As time went by, though, I began to miss my physical relationship with Julie. I sensed a distance from her that was disconcerting to me. Yes, we were bonded over our child, our perfect Bailey Jean, but we, as a couple, were not taking the time to be together, to work on our relationship. Like most parents, having children was a lot harder than I think we thought it would be. Our relationship certainly was not focused on sex anymore. We were mothers. But that wasn't the cause of our nonexistent sex life. We would go to couples therapy and we tried to work it out, but the sex wasn't coming back into the relationship. I am a very sexual being and sex is important to me in my relationships. I kept giving Julie the benefit of the doubt. I didn't want to push anything. I didn't experience giving birth to a child. I didn't know what that does to you. I've heard stories from lots of people; all my friends; their wives were having babies and they hadn't had sex in a long time either, so I kept thinking that it was common and just the way it was after having a baby. I thought that it would eventually come back. When I'd bring this up to Julie, she'd always say, "Give me space. Give me time." But I couldn't help but wonder: How much space? How much time?

That first year of Bailey's life was such an emotional roller coaster for me. I was so confused about Julie's needs and what she felt she wanted from me and our relationship together. On the other hand, the time I spent with Bailey was so profound. As the role of *mother* began to settle in more deeply with me, I couldn't help but look back at my own childhood, my own mother. Having a child is hard and, once you have one, there's a little bit more respect available for your own parents. This tiny crack in the door offered me the opportunity to talk to my own mother, to really try and deal with some of the things that had been so disturbing to me over the years. She and I are still not done with that process, but Bailey's birth definitely helped to open a bridge between us. At least we're *trying* now.

Julie began to talk about wanting another child. She'd always said she wanted to have two close together. I was still unsure of our relationship and what that would mean, but when Julie got something in her head, she went ahead and did it. So, as she began to make plans to inseminate again, I started to feel the need to write. I hadn't written any music in over two years—the longest I'd ever gone without writing. I began pulling out my notebooks, putting ideas down on paper. I was starting to write "Breakdown." And I had no idea how prescient that title would be.

My lyrics and my writing know a lot more about my life than I do. Up until the time I began the songs for my new album, *Skin,* my writing had tended to be ahead of my emotional and psychological consciousness. *Breakdown,* the album, as I discovered while writing this book, contained a lot of subconscious writing. Looking back on it, I am aware of what I originally had in mind when I wrote the songs. But from my perspective a few years later, it has become very clear to me that, in my creativity, I was allowing my emotions—what was happening in my life at that very moment—to come out as cleverly disguised (and sometimes not so cleverly disguised) metaphorical songs. I now know why that album was not really understood by critics or fans. It was crafted with contradictions and hidden messages. No wonder no one got it. I was terribly confused and my confusion is all over that album.

I was in New Mexico when I wrote the song "Breakdown." When I wrote the lyrics, I transcended myself back into a past experience. The song is about my decision to leave Kansas and drive to Los Angeles—at least, I thought it was when I wrote it. In retrospect, "Breakdown" was really about what was happening to my relationship with Julie. It was the same fork in the road that I had faced with other women in my life: my mother, my sister, Jane, Linda, Kathleen.

I got to a point, in all of these relationships, where they became too painful. They weren't filling me up in the way that I wanted. They were actually causing me more damage because emotionally, they all became too hard to handle. In each case, I knew that the time had come to move on. The hardest relationship to admit that about, of course, was with Julie, because I had stayed for so long. But I knew that there was nothing left and we were staying together like plastic and stone. It could have fallen completely apart at any given moment. And I really believed that I would be okay alone, even if I stayed in my relationship. My life was unraveling, and driving is a metaphor that I have used in a lot of my songs, to represent leaving or running away. Sadly, for Julie, all of this past history was very much a part of who I am. It came with me as part of the overall package.

The end of the song is an image of driving out of Leavenworth and leaving that part of my life behind. On one hand, my life as I knew it was completely coming undone. On the other, I was about to go out into the world, to spread my wings and pursue my dream, and fly. "Breakdown" is about emotional collapse, the end of my relationships with each of the women who have had any significant impact on my psyche, and the most obvious one—to everyone but the songwriter, me—the total crumbling of my life with Julie.

BREAKDOWN

How could I stay
How could I breathe
There had to be more for me
Promises gone
Plastic and stone
I'm doing fine all alone

So you're having a breakdown
So you're losing the fight
So you're having a breakdown
And I'm driving and crying
Unraveled and flying
I'm coming to your breakdown tonight

I cannot run
I cannot hide
It came with me locked inside
The bough will break
Cradle will fall It only takes one call

So you're having a breakdown
So you're losing the fight

So you're having a breakdown
And you need me tonight
I found my place in this downtown
Salt air and yellow street lights
So you're having a breakdown
And I'm driving and crying
Unraveled and flying
I'm coming to your breakdown tonight

Not all the songs on that album were my subconscious working itself out through my music. There was one track that jumped right from the headlines. I couldn't help but write about it. In the fall of 1998, Bill called and told me that the U.S. women's soccer team wanted me to write a theme song for them. The United States was hosting the Women's World Cup that year, and Bill explained to me that it was going to be huge. I thought it was pretty cool that they wanted me to be involved and be connected to part of the event, so I agreed.

I asked John Shanks, my co-producer on *Breakdown*, to send over a sample of some really driving and intense drum loops. I wanted to write this really great, dynamic, forceful song—my version of "We are the Champions."

It was October seventh, 1998. Julie was pregnant with Beckett, and we were in the kitchen fixing supper. I was caring for Bailey and we were listening to the news. A story came on CNN about another brutal attack on a young gay boy in Wyoming. I was, like, "Oh God, what's happened now?" I went over to the television, turned up the volume, and listened with great sadness. The young man was hanging on to his life by a thread. It was so devastating. In my little cocoon, with my alternative family, I had been thinking I was a big gay rock star actually doing something to change the world. The news report was like somebody just dropped a huge brick in my kitchen.

My phone starting ringing. People asked me, "Did you hear what happened?" All I could think of doing was getting together with some of my other friends. Ellen DeGeneres was already organizing a trip to the Denver hospital where this innocent victim of such a violent hate crime lay waiting to die because of his sexuality. Of course, I am speaking of Mathew Shepard.

Julie was very, very pregnant and I didn't want to leave her by herself with Bailey. I was still feeling pretty guilty about being gone for most of her first pregnancy, so I chose not to join Ellen on her visit. It was hard to say no, because the attack was so very brutal—a sign that this kind of hatred toward the gay community still exists in this country.

I cried uncontrollably when Mathew Shepard died. It was a sad day in many ways. He was so young and innocent. He looked like Gary, one of my best friends in high school, who was gay and lived in Leavenworth just like me.

Later that night, I went into my office and I tried to write the soccer song. I picked a loop at first that sounded very "Here-we-go, women-winning." Shanks had sent me another loop that was really, really intense. I didn't even have a guitar with me. I just started singing "Scarecrow, crying—." This image of a scarecrow was in my head because the bicyclist who found the boy's body thought that it was a scarecrow in the field until he got closer and realized it was a young man. I started jotting sentences down. The words just came pouring out of me. Mathew Shepard was a student at the University of Wyoming. He was beaten, tied to a wooden fence outside Laramie, and left on the windblown prairie to die at the age of twenty-one—all because he was gay. The vision in my mind—that young man hanging on a fence, condemned to die in such a dreadful way—has never subsided. The words were powerful, but not nearly as intense as the violent images that were in my head. I wrote and wrote and wrote pages of lyrics for "Scarecrow."

I tried to get back to writing the soccer song, but every time I sat down to write a rah-rah women's song, I'd come up with more words and questions about why this terrible tragedy had occurred in the first place. I wrote vivid descriptions of how bloody he was. Tying him to a post made his death Christ-like, and I wanted to draw the comparison. Lyrics like, "They tortured you and burned you. They beat you and they tied you. They left you cold and breathing. And for love, they crucified you. I can't forget, hard as I try, this silhouette against the sky." I had never written anything so graphic as this song.

The news kept showing that piece of fence where Mathew's body was found, and to this day, I cannot clear that image out of my mind. "Waiting to die, wondering why." I can't imagine what was going through his mind while he hung there, like a helpless scarecrow, for eighteen hours, just waiting to be found and waiting to die. I wrote, "The angels will hold and carry your soul," with the hope that his soul left his body long before his last breath.

I was very clear in wanting this song to send a political message out there too. My son was just about to be born, and I could not imagine the pain of a mother losing a son like that. "This was our brother, this was our son. This shepherd young mild, this unassuming one."

We all gasped when we heard this story. I think that it really hit us square in the face because, as a nation, we say, "This can't happen here, we're all much too civilized." But it can and it does—every day.

"Where can these monsters hide?" I just wanted to shout out to the world: How could you not see this? We breed this. "They are knocking on our front door, they're rocking in our cradles, they're preaching in our churches and eating at our tables." We see them every day, these people who have so much fear of sexuality. They must have been brutalized themselves as children in such a dark way. But my heart told me that these two young boys who did this to Mathew are not themselves monsters. These are kids who go to school in Colorado and Wyoming and Idaho, and Anywhere You Live, USA. They're our children. These are not somebody else's children. *They're ours.* I'm not talking of only Mathew Shepard, either. These young misguided boys who killed him are also someone's children.

With that understanding, I wanted to try and comprehend forgiveness. I can't grasp that kind of pain, overwhelming grief, fear for life, and disbelief. I know the darkness and shame. Somewhere along the way, these kids became disaffected, dislocated, and deviant. They must lubricate their reasons to hate. They learn it and fester it and continue this dreadful cycle.

I tried to insert myself into the message so that maybe I could teach tolerance and understanding and acceptance and love for one another. The more people try to come at me from this place of hate, the more I want to reach out and say, "I love you." I wrote: "Those who would pollute me, I love you; destroy and persecute me, I love you. Desecrate and hate me, I love you." How can I break the chain?

I searched my heart and my soul. In my mind, I tried to find forgiveness. It would be a big step for our world to be able to say the only way to break it, the only way to understand that kind of evil is to stop punishing the offenders, and treat them. I can forgive. I can *comprehend*—I don't say *understand*. But I will not forget. We cannot forget. We as a nation cannot just say, "Oh, wasn't that bad," and push the archaic persecution of homosexuality—of sexuality—aside.

In the most stunning act of benevolence I have ever heard of, Mathew's parents brokered a deal for one of his killers to serve two life sentences just as the jury was to begin hearing testimony about whether he should be put to death. In essence, the Shepards spared the life of the man who stole their son's life. That is a testament to true human spirit.

In memory of Mathew Shepard, may we forgive but never forget.

SCARECROW

Showers of your crimson blood
Seep into a nation calling up a flood
Of narrow minds who legislate
Thinly veiled intolerance
Bigotry and hate
But they tortured and burned you
They beat you and they tied you
They left you cold and breathing
For love they crucified you

I can't forget hard as I try
This silhouette against the sky
Scarecrow crying
Waiting to die wondering why
Scarecrow trying
Angels will hold carry your soul away

This was our brother
This was our son
This shepherd young and mild
This unassuming one
We all gasp this can't happen here
We're all much too civilized
Where can these monsters hide?
But they are knocking on our front door

They're rocking in our cradles
They're preaching in our churches
And eating at our tables
I search my soul
My heart and in my mind
To try and find forgiveness
This is someone's child
With pain unreconciled
Filled up with father's hate
Mother's neglect
I can forgive
But I will not forget
Scarecrow crying
Waiting to die wondering why
Scarecrow trying
Rising above all in the name of love

Our son Beckett was born on November eighteenth, 1998. We called it thirty-six hours of labor. As with Bailey, Julie had gone into labor but she was not dilating. This time around, we had decided to have a hospital birth from the git-go. We chose a hospital closer to our new home. When she went into labor, Julie wasn't in as much pain as she was with Bailey. Again, the baby was putting pressure on Julie's spine, so when labor started, the doctors gave her a mild epidural. Julie was very clear that she intended to walk out of that hospital immediately after giving birth, so they didn't give her too many drugs. I actually helped Beckett come out during the delivery. I was helping to push up Julie's legs when she pushed him out, so I was right there when he was born. Both times, I cut the umbilical cord. I was right there. Beckett made a lot more noise than Bailey did when she was born.

Thankfully, our pediatrician was available to check out Beckett right after Julie gave birth. Beckett was born at ten-thirty in the

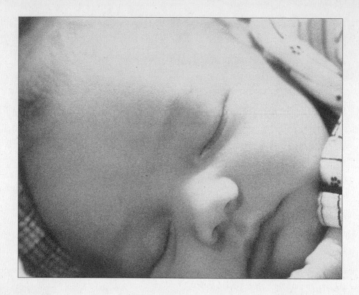

Beckett

Angel as a puppy on the road

*Grandma Etheridge
holding Bailey and
Beckett*

Bailey and me

morning, and Julie was on her way home by one-thirty in the afternoon. The nurses were great at this hospital. They told Julie that she could leave as soon as she ate, went to the bathroom, and had the doctor examine Beckett. The baby was fine, and he started breast-feeding right away. With that, Julie got up, went to the bathroom, ate, looked at me, and said, "Okay, let's go home."

Having a son was a completely different experience from having Bailey. I believe that children are born exactly who they are—that their personalities are intact at the moment of birth. And this little personality was completely different from Bailey. He was a *boy*, with all that out-there boy energy. This second child added a sense of completion to our little family. There were parents. There were siblings. We looked almost normal.

Except for Julie's and my deteriorating relationship. Once again, we were down that post-birth path of "Give me time. Give me space." It felt like it had before Julie got pregnant with Beckett. But there wouldn't be any more pregnancies to distract us now. Julie and I had to come head-to-head and really deal with our relationship, with our problems.

Because it always seemed that there was friction between us, Julie would get on my case about my weight, or how I dressed or that I wasn't helping out enough around the house. It was always something. I would try dressing a little sexier. I tried to do chores around the house. Nothing seemed to be working. No matter what I did, it was never enough.

So I went back into my "basement," I went into the studio to record *Breakdown*.

Breakdown

...

AFTER I HAD WRITTEN ALL THE SONGS FOR *BREAKDOWN*, Julie listened to them. She heard where I was coming from, what was going on in my head, and what I was creating musically. She came to me and said, "Well, it sure sounds like you're in a lot of pain and that I'm just this horrible person. It just sounds like there's so much going on. I dare you to write a love song." Never one to back down from a dare, I wrote the song "Sleep."

I have written many songs I am very very proud of, but I think that "Sleep" may be the most perfect song I have ever written. It's so sharp and small in scope. The first verse is about love and sex. The second verse is about building a home and moving into family life. And the third verse is about death. It's simple, poignant, and direct. A lot of my songs are shielded in metaphors and veils. I guess that's always been a safe way for me to reveal myself without feeling too exposed or vulnerable.

SLEEP

After your laughter like thunder
After your skin like coffee and cream
After it takes our bodies into the night
After we've come to the extreme

I want to lay down on your shoulder
Just inside your arm
I want to listen to your heart beat
And your breathing on and on
I want to lay down on your shoulder
Surrender to your peace
And go to sleep

And when we've gone a million miles
Made true our dreams with sweat and bone
After we've built it up with our bare hands
Made strong a place we can call home
And when the light in my eye is fading
When running water becomes too deep
Finally angels turn my fire to dust
And when my soul's no longer mine to keep

But as I kept working on the album, refining it to the point where I wanted it to be, it was getting harder and harder at home. This was supposed to be the time of my life. I had made it as a rock star. I had a big house, a fancy sports car, and a relationship that was a lot of work. I guess I expected all of that to fill the big, dark, empty black hole in my heart. I thought that Julie was supposed to make me feel safe. Every time I tried to communicate that, it didn't work. I thought that when I became a famous rock star, all of my problems would fade away. That's why I wanted to be famous in the first place: to solve my problems. I thought that being loved and adored by millions of people would surely fill up that deep, end-less pit I carry inside myself. I thought that I wouldn't be starved for that attention, affection, or redemption if I had the love of mil-lions. But I was. I was still emotionally malnourished. What was the missing piece? Why did I feel so continuously betrayed? I'd been with Julie for enough years to recognize that she needed to be on her own path and to understand her own darkened past. She needed filling up as much as I did. The problem was, I wasn't get-ting it from her, and she wasn't seeking it from me.

We continued going to our couples therapy class, and at least it helped us learn how to communicate better with one another. We learned how to share our feelings without placing blame or letting our own issues, our shadows, get in the way. We learned to convey our words directly about the issue at hand. Instead of saying, "You make me feel like this!" we learned to say, "When you say this, I feel sad, I feel hurt."

The real turning point for us came during a therapy session. Our therapist was trying to help us see that each of us was direct-ing blame toward the other. The therapist turned to Julie and said, "Julie, you're just blaming Melissa for this, you're blaming her for that. You're saying that it's all her fault. What about you?" I think that Julie felt cornered by the question and overwhelmed by her emotions. She was blaming me for whatever it was that I repre-sented in her life. Her response was a shocker. Julie turned to me and, instead of confronting her issues or admitting some blame, she said, "Well, I'm just not gay." I was devastated. This came out of nowhere. Ten years of a relationship, and she says to me that she's just not gay?

She said, "You know, I've tried, and I've tried these last cou-ple of years, and I'm just not gay." Ten years and two children later seemed like a bizarre time to make that discovery. What was I supposed to do with that? There was no place left to go. Those words destroyed me. They destroyed our family. What did this all mean?

Instead of storming out of the office, we started talking about what she meant exactly by telling me that she wasn't gay. I had a million questions. I wanted to know if it meant that we could still live together but we wouldn't have sex. What were the boundaries? Julie never said that she wanted to leave me. She never said that she wanted our relationship to be over. She wasn't even acknowledging her bisexuality at this point. She simply said that she was *no longer gay.*

This revelation came in the beginning of 1999. I was desperately trying to understand her. What I was hearing was that Julie was no longer attracted to me. That she was no longer attracted to women. She told me that, sexually, physically, she wanted a man. I wanted to know if she wanted to be married to a man or if she felt that she just needed a man's presence in her life. There was no answer to that.

By June 1999, we had made a decision that we would try whatever we could to save the relationship. At the end of six months, we would decide the fate of our future. In January 2000, we would make some choices.

In preparation for the release of *Breakdown,* I was scheduled to give a free concert in San Francisco in August. This was the first time I'd played live for a general audience in two years. They had been hard years. Having children, dealing with my deteriorating relationship with Julie. I was so looking forward to this concert. I needed response from an audience—a response that would fill me up and make me feel better about my life.

And for a few hours, it worked. I got out there and played hard. Maybe too hard. I was reaching, desperately trying to make myself feel better, to forget my problems and lose myself on stage. As the adrenaline of the show wore off and my emotions bottomed out again, I realized that the stage wasn't going to solve these problems for me. The only way these problems were going to be dealt with was by me. For me. It was a hard realization. One I'd been avoiding for many years.

Rolling Stone reviewed *Breakdown* on its release. It was the first time I felt that one of my albums got a really serious review. I'd always felt that, because I was sort of a singer *of* the people or *for* the people, I was not taken very seriously by critics. They even voted me Worst Singer in 1992. I'm not complaining; I have never been a critics' performer and I was never a cerebral songwriter. When *Rolling Stone* compared my song "My Lover" to "Mother," by John Lennon, I really drank that in and was grateful. I don't write my songs for the critics. Never have. But that was the ultimate compliment. It was just incredible. It was really, really something.

Lover Please

. . .

Of course, once the album was out, it was time to tour again. Julie and I had discussed it, and we thought the best choice for the four of us would be to go on the road together. To have the whole family traveling together. Beckett was about eight months old, Bailey was about two years. Before we left, I loved the idea. I thought it would be fun. Fun and easy, just hanging out and playing before the shows, before I'd go and perform.

I couldn't have been more wrong. Within days of starting the tour, it was clear that Julie seemed to feel like she was only out there to be the mom. Like she was just following me around. And she hated that. What I thought would be joyful and interesting for the kids turned out to be a drag. It was hard on them because they woke up in a different place every day, without the comfort and security of a constant home. Sure, their moms were there with them, but their moms were trying to figure out their own relationship as well. And I was tired. Tired all the time. Tours are arduous and I need downtime. But on this tour, the second I stopped working

My band and me just before takeoff: Kenny Aronoff, me, John Shanks,
and Mark Browne   © 1996 MELISSA ETHERIDGE/PHOTO BY NICOLE BENGIVENO / MATRIX

"You just landed on Park Place and it's mine! Pay up."

© 1996 MELISSA ETHERIDGE/PHOTO BY NICOLE BENGIVENO / MATRIX

I've got a lot on my mind. © 1995 MELISSA ETHERIDGE/PHOTO BY JODI WILLE

I had a child thrust into my arms, to deal with, to comfort. I had thought that having my family on the road would help me feel whole, give me a better understanding of how to deal with the problems Julie and I were having.

But the opposite happened. Everything in my life began to be more and more compartmentalized. Separate. There was the performing self. Who had nothing to do with the personal self. Who had nothing to do with the mothering self. There was no wholeness. Only parts of me. Pieces of me. I felt like I was being pulled in different directions all the time, never having a moment to sit down and say, "What do I want? What do I need?"

It was a dark time for me, that tour. I mean, I enjoyed myself on stage like I always do, but in some sense I was just going through the motions. Being so scattered, I felt that I couldn't fully commit myself anywhere. I was just searching—searching for a way to have it all make sense.

Julie and I tried everything. We both made an effort to see if we could somehow find that piece that had been missing the past few years. We talked about the idea of living together and not having sex. We talked about living together and not being monogamous. I had been here before. This is not what I wanted out of this relationship. I had already been through Julie's wanting and needing other people—men *and* women. What was driving her away? Was it me?

As the months went by, I had to start thinking about myself. I need passion in my life. I'll do a lot to stay in my relationships, but, at some point, I realized that I had been living without passion for the past couple of years. The idea that I would have a passionless existence for the rest of my life was unthinkable. The prospect of no attraction/no sex forever was something I could not fathom living with—even though it would mean keeping our family together.

I think that I deserve to be cherished and appreciated and loved. I tried taking sex out of the equation. Let's say that Julie and I were no longer going to be in a sexual relationship. We had spent eleven years together; we should be able to love each other. Maybe we could exist as best friends and keep our family intact. We had, after all, built a family together. Maybe I was putting too much emphasis on sex, and maybe it is not that important. Maybe if we found a bond as partners, I could accept this. But I couldn't even find affection. There was no kiss good-night. No hug hello. When we were sexually involved, I thought that those things existed. To me, sex is affection. I explained how I felt to Julie and asked her if we could try having an affectionate relationship that wasn't sexual. All I wanted was for her to say, "Good morning, hon," and hug me and kiss me. I really thought that if I got that from her, then maybe we could stay together and work out something else for each of us sexually. We tried that for a few weeks, but things weren't going as I had hoped. The weeks went by and it got to where Julie wouldn't even kiss me good morning. I guess, to her, a kiss in the morning meant sex, and she just wasn't going there. She couldn't differentiate between what I called affection and warmth and what she saw as sex.

We'd climb into bed at night and it was horrible. It was like an imaginary line had been drawn down the middle of the bed. Julie kept to her side and I was sure to stay on mine. She would read every night, and there was always a book between us—a boundary not to be crossed. I'd just get into bed and say, "Good night."

The kids turned out to be a tremendous source of warmth and affection for both of us during this time. When you have two kids, you're getting lots of love and yummies. We both got a tremendous amount of hugs and kisses, and the warm sensation that comes with the delight of holding and connecting with another human being. The kids and our animals filled that void in our lives for most of that time.

The new year was approaching and I had two weeks off from the tour. Julie and I decided to spend the time in our house in New Mexico, doing Christmas and ringing in the new year with the kids and some of our closest friends. There was a huge wall around Julie, and an enormous space was building between us. I barely felt that I knew her anymore. She was the woman I was very much in love with, the mother of my children, and I felt as if I couldn't touch her. The thought of my hand was too much for her to take. When I tried to show her some affection, she would tell me that I was making her feel uncomfortable. I told Julie that I had been giving our relationship a lot of thought and that I deserved someone in my life who would cherish and love me. I asked her if she thought she could be that person. She said, "No." It was Kathleen all over again. To me, that was it. We were over. This was not the way I had planned to ring in the new year, the new century, and the new millennium. I had so desperately hoped it would all bring a new beginning. I was crushed.

Oh, I cried, and cried, and cried, and cried, and cried, and cried. Inside, I was finally realizing that I deserved to be in love with someone who loved me back. My stand on my own self-esteem was that I deserved to be cherished, and loved, and kissed in the morning, and wanted. I am too young to settle for a loveless, sexless, passionless relationship. It's not even an age thing. I'm just not ready to quit all of that in my life. I think I can have that some-day—a belief I haven't felt for a very long time.

In a way, I was relieved that we had, at the very least, come to a mutual decision about our future. I told Julie that we'd figure everything out. I wanted her to be happy and I deserved to be happy too. We were still vacationing in New Mexico, and a couple days after our final confrontation, we got our friends Heather and Alex to babysit, and Julie and I went out to dinner. We had a few drinks and then decided to go to an Asian spa right outside of town. We liked to go there from time to time to get a massage, sit in one of the private Jacuzzis that are built in the trees, and relax in a pagoda. As bizarre as it seemed—I don't know, maybe I am a misogynist, maybe I was a little tipsy, whatever—it seemed right to head up there that night. It was the kind of setting that would surely induce an evening that would end in sex with a regular partner. This kind of night would normally be sexual. I was so confused. We drove home and, sure enough, we had wild, crazy, passionate sex— the kind we hadn't had in a very long time.

We had finally made a decision to break things off between us. Then, suddenly, I became attractive again to Julie. It was terribly confusing for both of us. I don't think either of us planned to wake up the next morning under these circumstances, but there we were. In each other's arms, feeling something that I thought had died a long time ago. Julie said that there was something in me that she hadn't seen in a long time—something attractive. And, well, maybe it wasn't that. Maybe it was something in me that was different.

I thought, "Wow! There is something there. But what the hell is it?" What was different this particular night that had been missing for the past three years? I thought that maybe she liked the independence I'd found. Maybe that's what she thought was new and attractive. We went home to Los Angeles, and we had sex for nine consecutive days. It was great. And it was crazy, and we were confused. It made me seriously question our earlier decision to split. Things were great, and I really don't know what made them that way. But when February reared its head, the walls started going up again.

In the midst of all of this unsettled emotional turmoil, I was busy trying to promote *Breakdown*. With this album, more than any other, I felt rather conflicted over the fact that my persona was bigger than my music. As I traveled around the world promoting and touring for the album, people would recognize me everywhere I went. They would tell me that I had made a difference in their lives, whether they were gay or not. What was really hard to take was the heavy focus on who the father of my children was. The attention wasn't about my music. I was interviewed by David Letterman, Jay Leno, and others, and the only thing anyone wanted to know was: Why wasn't I talking about who the father of my children is? It was all about this very private thing for Julie, my kids, and me, and the focus was all wrong.

The media love a good secret. There's a lot of power in possessing a secret like that. Personally, I have never liked secrets. It's not that I wanted to keep the identity of the father from anyone, I just believed that it was our personal business and no one else's. It drives people crazy not to know something like this. It's a natural curiosity. I don't blame anyone, but, frankly, it was no one else's business.

I realized that it was bigger than I thought it would be, and, sooner or later, Bailey might be approached by someone and asked about her daddy. I would lose my mind knowing that my daughter was vulnerable in that situation. There was a remote but slight possibility that something I'm not telling the world could actually harm my daughter in some way. That thought just made me crazy. Beckett was too young and not as vulnerable as Bailey when we chose to go public. Her well-being really concerned Julie and me.

The more interviews I did, the closer I got to telling the world. Letterman did a whole segment on the topic the night I was on, in 1998. Dan Quayle was on right before me. I came out, and the first thing David said to me was, "So who is the father of your kids? I'm no anthropologist," he said. "But, you got two women and two kids and there's something missing." The whole time I was on the show, this was all we talked about. Not my new album, which is why I was there in the first place. I like David Letterman. He has always been really kind to me. I use him as an example of how out of control the topic was getting. It was just spinning in a downward motion. He finally said to me, at the end of the last segment, "If I guess, will you tell me?" He's sitting there thinking. And all I could think of saying was, "All right, it's Dan Quayle." My answer got a big laugh and it was great fun, but I left there saying, "Damn. That's all I am now is a joke about who the father of my children is." This was not okay.

I'm proud of who the father of my children is. I don't want a secret hanging over my kids' heads. Right after Beckett was born, I saw Jann Wenner, the publisher of *Rolling Stone* magazine, at the "Concert of the Century" in Washington, D.C. in the late fall of 1998. I've known Jann for years. He was talking with me at the concert, and I threw out to him the following question: "What if I tell you who the father of my children is?" He looked at me and said, "Really?" And I said, "Yeah. Do you want to know? It's David Crosby." He was shocked and thrilled that I had shared this exclusive news with him. The truth is, it was time to reveal our last secret. I asked Jann if he wanted to print the truth in his magazine. He thought it was a spectacular idea.

When I agreed to do the *Rolling Stone* article, which was the first place we revealed that David Crosby, this musical legend, was the biological father, I was well aware that the issue was to be the first of the new millennium. It would display what the new American family looked like. It was a lifestyle statement. It was a political

David Crosby with my mom

Showing my appreciation to David on stage during a benefit concert in Ojai, California

© 1999 MELISSA ETHERIDGE/
PHOTO BY CATHERINE CASTRO

Jan, Julie, David, and me MARK SELIGER © 2001

statement. It was musical in nature because of David and myself, and it certainly was all of us standing in our truth. "Yup, this is what we did." I liked that we chose *Rolling Stone* as the place to share our story. It's a liberal magazine and there was no fear of someone going to interview the Reverend So-and-So about same-sex marriages and parenting. I knew that Jann would handle the story right. There was a certain safety in that knowledge for me.

Jann kept this supersecretive. He allowed only three people in on this covert mission. He wouldn't even tell the people in his office. Jancee Dunn did the interview with the Crosbys and me, and Mark Seliger took the photographs. Everyone thought it was going to be a Mariah Carey cover. Jann kept the pictures secret. He didn't want anyone to have a jump on his story. I thought that the article was great and very open, even though, behind the scenes, Julie and I were still in the midst of deciding whether we had a future as a couple. If you read the article, there's a few lines of, "You know, I don't know about the future. Relationships are hard; who knows what's going to happen? It's a lot of hard work." That was also the last line of our *60 Minutes II* interview with Charlie Rose. (Pretty perceptive producers on that show!) If you really look at those two interviews, you'll see a little seeping through of what was going on with me—with us.

During subsequent interviews, everyone tried to point out how perfect things seemed in my life. I kept denying that things were perfect. I did an *Advocate* interview. "It's not perfect, it's not all rose-colored glasses." It was right there in front of everyone's face. And my new album was shouting to the world. Songs like "Enough of Me," "My Lover," and "Stronger Than Me" speak to the problems in my relationship with Julie. I didn't even recognize the connection or admit to it until I started writing this book. It was a very dark time in my life—a time shrouded in all kinds of denial and desperation.

The revelation of David Crosby's fatherhood became a source of unending comedic fun. All of the late-night talk shows took a turn at poking fun at us. I knew that we had penetrated the core of the debate on the issue of same-sex parenting, but I didn't have any clue as to how deep inside the American—and even the global—consciousness we had gone. I thought it would be a little ping on the radar screen and then would dissipate. I was somewhere in Germany during my last European tour, and I couldn't sleep. I was jet-lagged, so I turned on the television. The Academy Awards were on. Billy Crystal, who was hosting, was spoofing *The Sixth Sense,* telling different actors and actresses in the audience that he could read minds. He went up to Michael Duncan Clarke, the big guy from *The Green Mile,* and said, "I see white people." Big joke; ha ha ha. He saw Annette Bening, who was very pregnant, and he said, "I hope it doesn't look like David Crosby." Even my friend Ellen DeGeneres milked it for her red-carpet gig during the Grammy Awards that year. She was standing on the red carpet, interviewing all of the people coming in. She was holding a plastic cup and asking for any donors.

I didn't mind the jokes; mostly, they were funny. It was crazy and wacky. David has a colorful past anyway, so he was used to it. A comic strip in *The Toronto Sun* projected a Grammy acceptance speech in the year 2050. It was captioned "The Sons of Crosby" and pictured seven little David Crosbys, with big thick mustaches and balding heads, standing on a stage. They were holding their Grammys and thanking their mom, Melissa Etheridge, and their dad, David Crosby. I actually saved that one.

The End

...

BIRTHDAYS ARE HUGE FOR ME. THEY ALWAYS HAVE BEEN. I had my first romantic kiss with a woman on the night of my seventeenth birthday. I moved to Los Angeles on my twenty-first birthday. I swore I'd be signed to a record contract by my twenty-fifth birthday. I never wanted to be the kind of person who moped around on my birthday. I am "Miss Celebrate-Your-Birthday." After my eighteenth birthday debacle, when my birthday was just forgotten, I decided that I was never going to go through that kind of disappointment on my big day again. Just to make sure that I have fun on my birthday, I throw a big party for myself every year.

My thirty-ninth birthday was coming around, and I realized that I wasn't happy—not at all. I usually have my astrological chart done every year around my birthday, and that year the astrologer told me that things were going to be insane. She said that my thirty-ninth year was a year of change. All of my planets were lined up and though the years leading up to this one seemed to be sort of slow and boring, my thirty-ninth was going to change all of that. Boy, did it ever!

I remember being in high school and figuring out that in the year 2000, I would be thirty-nine years old. I wondered where I would be and what I'd be doing. As far back as I can remember, I had dreamed of becoming a rock star. Somehow I knew that I would be on stage. I am more comfortable there than I am anywhere else. The stage feels like home to me. I thought that if I could become a famous singer, all of my problems would be solved and I'd be so happy. And I'd fulfilled those dreams. I couldn't go out in public without being recognized. I had five platinum albums. Someone called me "America's foremost female rock 'n' roller." I had everything. Except a relationship. As my thirty-ninth birthday snuck up on me, it was time to admit my personal life was in a shambles.

Julie and I had gotten to a point where we couldn't even say "good night" to each other. All of our emotional walls were up— way up. Our therapist had said that we had gone through a cycle of approaching and avoiding. Meaning, "I only want you if you are not available, and if you're available, you're not attractive to me anymore." We had had years of this kind of back-and-forth emotional pull. I'd be, like, "You want to be together, then here I am. Okay, now you don't want to be together, so I'll just go away for a while. Oh, you want me again because I am away? Okay, then, I'm back." It became a vicious cycle for both of us. Our therapist could pinpoint exactly where we were in our cycle on any given day. She knew our pattern like it was mapped out on a graph. It became completely exhausting for us. I kept going around and around that damn track. I knew that I would have to remove myself from the pattern in order to see things more clearly. And in May of 2000, I finally did.

Julie had been so distant leading up to my birthday. I just thought to myself, "Well, this sucks. I'd rather be alone than wishing for something I will never have in this relationship." All I could see was that my partner wasn't looking at me anymore. At my birthday bash, a few days before the actual date, Julie and I had pretended that everything was fine. And I did have fun. Dancing. Body shots. Tequila and cake with all my friends. It was exactly the kind of party it should have been. But, clearly, Julie wasn't sharing it with me.

When I woke up on the morning of my birthday, Julie wouldn't even kiss me. She was so distant. I just sat on the back patio, played with the kids, and felt so alone. And *whammo*! I had an awakening like I had never had before. I decided right there and then that it was time to get off that track. To pull out. The night of my birthday, I decided that I was through. I was no longer going to look out for Julie's interests over my own. For the first time in our relationship, I put what was good for myself over anything and everyone else. If I wanted to know how I looked, I would have to look in the mirror. If I needed affection, I would find a way to love myself. If I lost weight, I would do it for me.

I woke up the morning after my birthday and thought about what my new life was going to look like. Julie and I were still living together, but that was all we were doing together. That afternoon, I went out and bought myself new clothes. Clothes I liked. Things I felt good in. I was dressing for me for the first time in years.

I no longer felt this need to be committed. I wanted to find someone to connect with and, frankly, just fool around with. A week after my birthday, I had to go to Atlanta for a solo performance. The first night I was there, I went out with a guy friend of mine and, for kicks, we decided to go to a straight bar. It was there that I met a gal, a beautiful blonde, Britney Spears look-alike, wearing this funky cowboy hat. She saw me across the room, and I looked at her and said, "Give me your hat." I snatched it right off her head and put it on. We ended up going out all night long, her and her friends and me and mine. We went to a strip club. I'd never been to one! I was, like, "Whoa. I missed out." And of course the girls in the club recognized me and all of them wanted to dance at our table. It was a crazy good time. The truth is, I wasn't all that turned on by it. I can imagine that for a guy it would be really great, but for me there was no emotional attachment. It was all very physical. Oh, I enjoyed the attention. I liked having every dancer come up and ask me to do a shot with them or just dance in my face. The funny thing was: I didn't have any money on me. The owner of the club gave me money to tip the dancers. It was just crazy. They were paying me to be in the club!

Why should I deny myself? Yeah, I wanted to keep my family together, but this physical issue was a very big part of our decision to split. It's a big part of who I am, and I'm not interested in not having this in my life.

I came home and I told Julie everything. She hated hearing it. I informed her that I intended to spend my summer having a good time and getting myself together. And, once again, my pulling away started the cycle that Julie and I had become so very good at. The further I stepped out of the relationship, the more she wanted me. Suddenly I was desirable again, because I was on my own independent path.

We had done it too many times before, but we came back together yet again. We tried to make it work with the understanding that we would be together—that is, our family would be together in the same place, but we would be nonmonogamous.

I was not enjoying the new arrangement, even though Julie and I had started to connect on a physical level again. This pattern simply could not continue because it was not good for either of us. I started to wind things down again by the end of July. By August, I was back on my own path. I was no longer available to her on an emotional level because I was putting it inside myself.

At one point, Julie came to me and said that she wasn't happy with the way things were going between us. She wanted to work on our relationship. I had to explain to her that, from my perspective, *we* were not in *our* relationship anymore. I was off on my own, working on me, and I wanted Julie to work on herself. I thought that if she could commit to having a healthy, monogamous relationship—something we were thinking might be possible in the future—then I would agree to work on our relationship sometime in the future. But, for the moment, we no longer had our relationship, so I told her no.

I think that threw her a curve she wasn't expecting because that arrangement wasn't part of the routine we'd fallen into. She quickly stepped up to the plate and tried to convince me that we could have a monogamous, healthy relationship and that she was through with her need for men.

She was finally saying what I'd been waiting to hear for years. But her words were only words. From that minute on, her darkness, resentfulness, and restlessness returned. She seemed so miserable. We were fighting every day. She was as far away from me as anyone could get. And every day it was something else. I'm not [this] enough, I'm not [that] enough.

About two weeks went by, and I realized that this was a miserable, horrible way to live. Julie called a friend who was in group therapy with us and asked for intervention because Julie and I were at a point where we couldn't even speak to each other without an argument ensuing. We all decided to meet at a park near our home and talk. Julie and I started by trying to communicate with each other and deal with our issues. It was the same old place in our relationship that Julie and I had visited a thousand times. I guess she felt cornered again because she pulled out her "I'm just not gay" below the belt punch for the *final* time.

I couldn't bear to hear that one more time. That was it—I was not dealing with this issue anymore. I wasn't going to let her toy with me and take that easy way out. If that's where she was going to take things, then I was through. This time, it was over. I never ever wanted Julie to be something she was not. I might never know, but I just don't believe that's the whole story. I think it became an easy door. Where was I supposed to go and what was I supposed to say after she told me something like that?

I had this sinking feeling that my life was in an uncontrollable downward spiral after we agreed to separate. The day I told my manager, Bill, that Julie and I were separating, was the day I felt that we had bottomed out. He had come to the recording studio and he was taken completely by surprise. This man has been in my life for nearly twenty years. He has seen a lot of people come and go, but this time it was different. Even though he understood, I knew that I would soon have to face the daunting task of telling all of the people I loved. Up to this point, no one knew anything about the breakup. I hadn't talked to anyone about it. And that was hard to do because I was about to go to Julie's thirty-sixth birthday party—a night of celebration with all of our friends.

We agreed to be respectful of each other at the birthday party. I wasn't going to go hunting down somebody and neither was she. I just wanted to get through it. But it was horrible. I spent the whole night shying away from Julie, pretending to everyone that everything was just fine. It was a lie and I was telling that lie in a room full of the people I loved the most.

The next day, we began to discuss how we were going to tell everyone. Our decision to break the news to our friends and family came quicker than we had anticipated. *The Star* was going to break the story in its next issue, so we had less than twenty-four hours to make our calls. I have no idea how *The Star* found out, but we had to call everyone we knew and tell them that we were breaking up. That was extremely hard. We couldn't get into details with anyone because of the time issue, so we just let everyone know that this was happening and we'd talk about it later. We didn't want any of our closest friends to learn about it from the morning paper.

The hardest call was to David and Jan Crosby. Julie and I felt we had let them down. This wasn't what they had in mind when they gave us their gift. I'll never forget their reaction. It was from their heart. They said, "It was a gift. It didn't come with any conditions." They assured us that they had all of the trust in our abilities, as parents, to make the right decision for our children. All they wished for was the best for Julie and myself. We've actually seen them more since the breakup than we did before.

As crazy as it sounded, and as hard as it was to find, Julie and I decided to find two homes that we could move into that shared a common yard space, because neither of us was willing to lose a moment with our children. Our idea was revolutionary in terms of an amicable separation. Our main concern was for the children's well-being. We talked with our therapist, who told us that, in a perfect world, parents would have to go from house to house and children could stay put. But the reality of that circumstance was not feasible, nor desirable, so we discussed it and agreed to get back-to-back homes. We could then put in a gate so the children would feel they could come and go through the yards anytime they wanted.

Shockingly, Julie found the perfect homes very quickly. Exactly the ones we wanted. And so we began to plan our move—something I was looking forward to, but something that was actually much more painful than I would have liked to admit.

Packing up "our" house and dividing "our" stuff was the hardest, lowest, shakiest, most frightening part of the process for me. It was a slow ripping-apart of our twelve years together. I can't even tell you how hard that packing situation was. You start packing things up, and ask, "Is this yours or is it mine?" Going through the CDs, "This is your music, this is my music," Even talk of "Your house, my house" was hard to swallow. The dirt in the house just kept getting thicker and thicker as the boxes were packed and things came off the walls. This wasn't just the dismantling of our home, it was the dismantling of "our" life.

I felt like I couldn't breathe. I'd always thought of a house as a metaphor for life, and here was mine coming apart day by day. I could barely sleep. I couldn't eat. I just felt sick. Twelve years of my life were being boxed up and taken away before my eyes. And then the hot water heater in the attic exploded. Water poured through the ceilings into the house, drenching everything, just like it was raining inside.

We were moving. And our house was crying.

skin

...

I'D STARTED WORKING ON *SKIN*, MY NEW ALBUM, BEFORE
we had moved out of the old house. Making this record was a completely different recording experience than I had ever had. The studio became my refuge during the breakup and the move into the
new house. After I'd get up and spend some time with the kids, I
couldn't wait to get there in the morning and pour every ounce of
energy and thought and emotion I had into the making of the
album. I would walk into the studio and I'd shut the door, leaving
all the turmoil of my life behind me with a huge sigh of relief. I'd
get lost in the songs. It was like when I was ten years old and running into my basement to write songs. Everything was dark and
filled with hurt and fear. It was a time of tremendous hurt. Except
this time, the "basement" was the recording studio. I just put all of
that emotion into my new songs. My heart would just pound. I
couldn't eat anything but chicken taquitos. And I would just
sing . . . and let it out. Almost all the vocals on the album were
recorded in their first take, live.

© 1995 Melissa Etheridge/Photo by Jodi Wille

Recording
Your Litle Secret.

© 1995 Melissa Etheridge/Photo by Jodi Wille

In the studio making Your Little Secret

David Cole, John Carter, and me in the studio making Skin

I worked with producer David Cole, who is the sweetest, gentlest, most un-Hollywood guy. He's a total family man. He was just so *there* with me. He was always interested in what I was doing, and where I was at with my songwriting, and he encouraged me to go deeper—to search inside myself and grab hold of all of the emotional stuff that was stirring. David was great. He'd laugh at all of my jokes, and we'd say really corny things to one another. I felt like I grew up with him.

The studio became a safe place. Steven Girmant was in the other room, and between him and David, I felt completely protected from the outside world. Had I been working with people I felt guarded with, I'm not sure they would have gotten the results that David did. I hadn't told David that Julie and I were having problems when we first started recording the album. The day I went in and spilled the beans, he just looked at me and said that he figured something was up because of the songs. We were really connected and I think it's been key in making this album so real and so of-the-moment. There were no judgments on the material. He started off working with this very broken baby bird and he gently nursed me through my catharsis. I could say, do, and be whatever I felt, and he'd help me make it into music. Even when David would send me back into that painful world and tell me to write deeper, I would step back and create images that were so much better than what I started with.

I wrote a lot of thoughts that never became songs for this album. There were moments of self-pity, anger, grief, and emancipation. Though I do not consider myself to be a poet—poets are much more accomplished than I am—I am a lyricist, and while writing the songs for *Skin*, I let my creative juices start to flow so that I could get that thought process and my brain working again. I had not written a song for well over a year.

I want a drink, a real one, nothing fancy or smooth, vodka or gin,
 some excuse for being rude.
I want to sit at the end of the bar and think and drink.
I want someone to ask me to dance just so I can turn them away.
When I get good and drunk, then I'll dance.
But until then, this misery stays.
I want the bartender to tell me a story about
How Elvis just showed up here one night.
And there's a napkin he signed on the wall
 and a bullet hole just to the right.
And I don't want to make any sense.
And I don't want to figure it out.
I don't want you to find me and come in and remind me.

That was as far as I got on that, but I kept coming up with lines like "The heart is a garden you dig your fingers in," and I would sit down with these drum loops and try to pour it all out on paper. Usually, I would just sit with my guitar, but this time my inspiration was coming from a new rhythmic source. It helped me a lot in the process because I could hear the beginning of a song in my head and then work with the drum loops to create from my feelings. The first song I wrote for the album was "Down to One," which was also written as just lyrics. I read it to a friend, and her reaction wasn't to reel from the pain of the song. She understood it, and that helped me keep going, because my life was definitely changing. It was completely different, and I think a lot of people have experienced, at some time in their life, all of the feelings I was writing about. My songwriting was wonderfully therapeutic for me.

Aside from the emotional rescue of the songs, making *Skin* involved a lot of first-time creative musical experiences in the studio. I wanted to make an album where I did everything. I played every instrument and sang all of the tracks. We'd start off by putting down a rhythm track with a drum loop, and then I'd play acoustic guitar. And then I'd sing. And David would start to build these layers of tracks that became my songs. Usually, when I record, I sing the entire song three times and then the producer and I pick the version we like best. David used to call my singing his favorite time of the day because it was filled with so much passion and emotion straight from my gut. Even though there are flaws in some of the songs, we decided that performance was more important than perfection. I would later bring in Kenny and Mark to add live drums and bass to help some of the songs.

David and I experimented a lot with sounds and instruments and vocals. I'd tell him, "I want a spooky sound," and he'd find it for me. John Carter, who was the executive producer of the album, came to the studio one day to check on me and on our progress. One of the last things Carter said before he left the studio that day was, "Whenever you're stuck and you want to try to do something with an instrument, use your voice." I wasn't really sure what he was trying to say, but I went back into the studio after he left, and started layering harmony and dissonance. We built layers of color behind the songs. One of the last songs we finished was "It's Only Me," and I wanted to have this moment in the song, right before the very end, where you hear the sound of insanity. We called it "the moment." David suggested that I go into the studio and just let out a very impassioned tribal OH GOD! scream. What is heard in the final mix is that scream played backward. It was the last thing I did vocally for the album, and it was a final purge of everything that had been building up inside me during the making of *Skin*.

I really love this album. It was exactly what I needed to get me through those first few months after breaking up with Julie. I needed it to move through this transition. It's also the first album I have written that is about a specific moment in time. It's not a smattering of songs from different periods of my life. I cannot wait to perform the songs from this album live in concert.

As the record came together, I slowly became more comfortable in my new house with its unique closeness to my ex. It became a comfort to me in that I would see my children and that would be in close range to me. That gave me hope that everything could be worked out so that Julie and I would both be happy. Our parental lives are very closely intertwined, but it's still a struggle to separate our personal lives when we live so close to each other.

I'm discovering how much I like living alone. I've decorated my house exactly the way I wanted to. That's something I'd never done. I bought myself a flat-screen TV, which is something I really wanted. If I leave something on the kitchen counter, it's still there the next day.

I am starting to put into myself everything I'd been giving away. I have opened my eyes to the rest of the world. When I see Julie, I see a person I've known for a long time. Attractive, yes. But that desire is no longer there. And I think that desire came from feeling like she was a piece of me, and if I didn't have that piece, I'd be missing something. There'd be an emptiness.

Having since shared passion with other women, in a very simple and very noncommittal way—women who find me attractive, who say "Look at how good your stomach looks," and "You're beautiful," you know, just very simply giving of themselves, with no expectations—I am sure that I could never go back to anything less. I'm planning on moving on and finding someone who's at a different place in her life. Someone who is on her own journey and is ready for a relationship full of giving and receiving.

I wanted to find a way to celebrate this new me, this new woman who was emerging from the ashes of the old. I'd wanted a tattoo for years, but I could never decide exactly what to ink on my skin forever. Then I met a woman who was a wardrobe stylist on a photo shoot I was doing, and she had a white tattoo that I thought was really cool. A white tattoo uses white ink. The image is faint but it's really pretty. Not only would I get a tattoo, but it would make a great picture.

I called a photographer, Dan Winters, and talked to him about my idea. I decided to tattoo the back of my neck, a place on my body that I never see, and I asked Dan to photograph it for me. I went to Graffiti Palace, a tattoo parlor in North Hollywood. White tattoos are rare, and this apparently was the only place in town that had an artist—Abel—who specialized in white tattoos. When I called to make an appointment, Abel told me to come down at nine P.M. My mom was scheduled to come to town later that week, so to actually go through with this, tonight had to be the night. I contacted Dan to be sure that he could make it, and he said he'd be there. I had dinner with a friend, drank some sake, and went to the San Fernando Valley so I could get my tattoo.

I sat with my back to Abel and put my head down so he could have a clean line on my neck. Abel was a real heavy-metal-looking dude. He was tattooed on every visible part of his body. Everyone in the shop had the same sort of look. There was nothing Hollywood about the place. It was real, and they took their craft every bit as seriously as I do mine. We designed how it was going to look and then he made a stencil of it, which he used to create the outline for the tattoo. It hurt, but in sort of a good way. It was sexy and exciting. I can understand how people would get turned on by the pain of the whole process and would want to tattoo their bodies all over. The rush kind of hurts, but it takes your mind to a whole new place that is almost a pleasure. Abel had a power over me that I found exciting in every way. I wasn't Melissa Etheridge, "Rock Star"; I was his canvas. My skin belonged to him for those few moments. And it was my choice alone to surrender that over to another person. It was a mind trip that made my head spin.

The entire process took about ten minutes. As Abel worked, blood slowly seeped to the surface, and the word *skin* was visible in my own blood. I became hyper-aware of this spot on my body that I had never given a second thought to before this moment. But I do now. I know it's there. It was a strange and wonderful sensation. The best part of the process for me was at the end. As Abel put his final touches on my tattoo, he put his hand on my shoulder and whispered quietly into my ear, "Congratulations. Now you are one of us."

It so struck me when he said that. The only community I was used to being accepted by was the gay community. I'd drive through West Hollywood and stretch my arms out wide, saying, "My people!" But here was a guy about as different from me as you could get: "Headbanger's Ball" on the tube, heavy metal blaring through the shop, and here he was welcoming me into his community with open arms. It was like a door being opened. Making me realize how much I'd been putting myself into a box—I'm this, I'm that . . .

Not anymore, I'm not. No more boxes. Not for me.

The Beginning

. . .

IN THE PAST, I'VE ALWAYS HOOKED UP WITH SOMEONE else's energy, but these days I'm getting to know myself. I used to spend a lot of energy trying to figure out what I was supposed to do for somebody else. I used to feel a pull on me. When I've been in relationships, I've put pressure on myself: I am supposed to be doing this or that, rather than doing what I wanted. That kind of thinking takes me right back to being ten years old. There's someone telling me what to do, shaping what I look like and how I act. These days, I've taken over those responsibilities for myself and I am standing on my own two feet—I think, for the first time in my life. Amid all of the stress and pain and insanity, there's a newfound excitement for discovering *me*.

For the most part, I was content with giving over all of that control to someone else. When I was busy doing my work, I didn't have to worry as much about all of those things. I'm starting to realize just how much of myself I gave away. The energy I was putting out in my relationships I am now putting into my children and

STEPHANIE PFRIENDER © ISLAND RECORDS, INC., 1995

STEPHANIE PFRIENDER © ISLAND RECORDS, INC., 1995

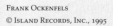

me. I have that energy for myself now. I am learning to draw better boundaries now than I ever have before. You get used to dancing with someone for so many years. You know what moves that person's going to make. You can follow the steps very easily. But that is not what a relationship is all about. You get compliant. And toward the end of my relationship with Julie, I wasn't really angry. I think that I was bitter. I resent the way the past few years of our life together unfolded.

We need to maintain some kind of rapport because of the children. We had to find a way to get along and communicate as co-parents. Julie is going to be in my life forever. That's the reality of my situation. That's my truth. Finding this common ground hasn't been easy for either of us. I think that I am still numb about the whole breakup. I don't feel a burning anything.

For the first time in my adult life, I am discovering who I really am. It's been hard to get used to being a single woman. I've never really been single and surely not since I became famous. I went to the *Proof of Life* movie premiere with Laura Dern, Rosanna Arquette, and Meg Ryan—all of whom I consider my close friends. It was one of the first social things I did alone after announcing my breakup with Julie. Someone had asked me whether I felt comfortable because I always had the comfort and security of having Julie with me at this kind of Hollywood event. The truth is, I was not comfortable, but I liked that I wasn't. I enjoyed feeling that way because, for the first time in a very long time, I felt *me*. Melissa the woman—the caring, feeling, emotional woman that I am becoming. It was the first time that I stood in front of the paparazzi line and had my picture taken as one, not half of one. I felt it was the beginning of a redefining of who I am. I came away from the night with a feeling of wanting to get to know myself better. In a strange way, I was transcended back to high school. Here I was at this big movie premiere, sitting with these huge stars and talking to them, and everyone is talking about "he said/she said" kind of stuff, and it was everything I had gone through in high school. It was the same old stuff but the people were better dressed! But, unlike high school, I felt very strong and more confident in my aloneness. My independence has been surprisingly empowering. I'm almost dizzy from how quickly things are changing in my life now that I am on my own.

I feel like I am relearning everything. I think this nervous excitement will overflow into my performances on stage. I feel like people know more about me now than ever before. When I go on tour this time, it'll be the first time that I will be standing completely in my truth, not in some creative version of my life that I disguised in my music for as long as I have been composing. I've always been a good storyteller, but I had maintained a certain level of control, in terms of just how much of the story I would share through the songs. As truthful as they were, a certain amount of illusion was always generated. This time, when I get out on stage, everyone will know the whole story—the reality of what's been happening in my life.

My new album, *Skin*, is filled with music that has never been closer to my core. And this time, when I get out there and sing songs like "Come to My Window" and "I'm the Only One," each word will hit a little harder because I will be more exposed in every way. I've been wounded before, but I've never been as connected as I was in this last relationship. There's never been this giant magnifying glass held over my life after the end of a relationship.

It's all so new, and I feel more vulnerable than I have in the past. When my circumstances changed, so did my truth. That's just the way it works. Maybe it'll turn out to be a better one than it was? Who knows?

The first step in my catharsis after breaking up with Julie was to come to the realization that I can have the loving one-on-one partnership I have been looking for my whole life. When I first started writing this book, I had no immediate plans to go on tour. I planned to be home with my family. The prospect of recording a new album wasn't even a thought in my head. I had been preparing to do a one-woman show on Broadway, and I had resolved to myself that I would probably never have all that I desired from my relationship—and I was willing to roll over on that need.

Fast forward to ten months later. It's 2001 and I have changed my tune on almost all of the above. The biggest epiphany is that I want to be in love and I believe that I will someday find what I've been looking for. I believe that I will find someone who is strong on her own and is grounded and won't need validation from me, and I won't seek it from her. I want to be able to experience being big old loud Melissa. No judgments, no excuses. I want to wear my old cowboy boots and feel comfortable about who I am on the inside and out. I deserve a relationship with someone who is as in love with me as I am with her.

But I'm a mom now, so any relationship I'm going to have has to be balanced against that. The days when everything fell by the wayside for whoever my newest love might be are long gone. Because when I wake up in the morning, I've got two other souls to contend with, to nurture, to love. All that I have been seeking throughout my life I am now free to give to my own children—all of the love, affection, warmth, attention, security, safety, and communication that my journey has lacked. I am now in a position to propel their lives forward so they never have to ask why they didn't get any of this. They're a lot of work, but my two children are the most incredible thing that's happened in my life. My breakup with Julie was hard. It was a new beginning for all of us. And even if my personal issues are still there, they're less pressing. Children clarify things; they make the choices one has to make more obvious. I want to enjoy every day of this trip I'm on and share it with my two fabulous children, Bailey and Beckett.

I'm not naïve. I realize that my children will face a set of challenges that other kids they grow up with will never know. I know that my children will be approached about having two mothers. They'll be faced with answering questions about my alternative lifestyle. They might be teased about their famous mother. I hope they won't, but it's possible. As a mother, I want to try to protect them from anything bad that might come from my celebrity or my sexual preference. I would never want to be the cause of any pain for either of them. For me, their happiness and well-being weigh is a little higher on the scale of priorities than anything else. I am who I am, and that's not going to change. All I can hope to do is teach my children about tolerance and understanding. I will always be honest with them about whatever they want to know.

Bailey came to me last year and wanted to know why she couldn't have a daddy who lived in the house, like some of the rest of her friends. She said that she didn't want David to be her daddy because he doesn't live with us. I had to think carefully about how to answer her. I explained that even though David is her dad, he gave us a very special gift, and he doesn't live in our house so that I can live here. My amazing daughter just looked at me and said, "Oh, okay." And has never brought it up again. I am so glad that I found the answer to that question. I'm sure there will be many others down the road. I hope I will be able to gently guide them along the way. My children certainly know that they have a life filled with unconditional love.

Because I am always putting my personal life out there in the universe through my music, I know that my kids are going to start

The safest, most perfect place I know

© 1996 Melissa Etheridge/Photo by Nicole Bengiveno / Matrix

© 1996 Melissa Etheridge/Photo by Nicole Bengiveno / Matrix

asking me questions about who I am and where some of these things come from. They'll want to know how to get through life. What am I supposed to do to handle all of the curves? I want to encourage my kids that they can do anything they choose, be anything they desire. If they can imagine, they can make their fantasies a reality. Bailey and I were driving in my car and she was telling me that she really, *really* wants to fly. She said, "I know that I can get into an airplane and fly, but I want to fly without being in an airplane. I want to fly like a bird or a butterfly or a plane." I answered by asking her how she thought she could do that. I didn't want to say to her, "Nope, you can't fly." End of dream. I want her to feel shat she is a free spirit with endless possibilities and no limitations.

At the end of the day, none of it—being famous and a gay role model; the political issues, the positive force, the music, the success—none of that compares to the happiness and love I have for my kids. Other things are completely secondary and do not even come close to their health, security, and happiness. They have helped me put my life into perspective. I am truly blessed by them, and I thank God every day for them. Being a parent is a wonderful blessing. The times that I have chosen to be truthful and stepped up are the times when I have been lifted up and moved up spiritually and emotionally. If I pass only one thing on to my children, I want them to know, have, respect, and understand the truth.

A TRUTHFUL LULLABY

How can I tell you of a world
That's changing right in front of me
How can I give you to a world
That's taken every breath from me

Who are these, these strangers
That cannot tell the love from lies
How can I send you to a world
Without a truthful lullaby

And when you find that what you seek
Is a conscience not within their minds
You slay the dragons as they sleep
Your souls are reluctantly entwined
Your brothers your sisters
Will race your dreams across the sky
I hope you find that what you seek
Is only a truthful lullaby

How can I tell you of a world
That's changing right in front of me
How can I give you to a world
That's taken every breath from me
And all I can give you
Is all I've learned in my own time
And so I send you to the world
With only a truthful lullaby

Afterword

...

It's been a full year since I finished this book. A year as exciting and invigorating and terrifying as any I've known. So much of the year has felt like a long, steady climb out of a dark hole. After the breakup with Julie I spent more time alone than I ever have. The kids would be spending time with Julie and I'd wander my new house all by myself. I think I made a conscious effort not to fill up my time in the ways that I used to. I could have called friends, gone out, tried to pretend that things were okay. But things weren't okay. And I really wanted to *feel* that, live with that feeling rather than pretend it wasn't there. It wasn't lonely, really, but it was alone. I think I was trying to gather myself together, my strength. I knew that eventually I'd look back on that time and think about how hard it was, but I also knew that if I was ever really going to get past it, move beyond it, then I had to really experience all those feelings, all those emotions, so I could truly move on without carrying any of that baggage with me.

In some sense, the book you've just read was the culmination of all my attempts to move on. I put my whole life down in one place . . . all my thoughts, fears, emotions, and problems, all in an attempt to move forward. To be new again. I wanted to cut loose from all the ties that bound me and enter the world fresh.

The problem with being fresh, of course, is that people suddenly take a new look at you. I've been in the public eye for many years now, but it was always *my* choice what people knew and when they knew it. The book changed all that.

One of my first interviews for the book was with a reporter from an English newspaper. She'd flown in to Los Angeles from

London and had read the galleys for the book on the flight over. She showed up at my house, and I walked into the room ready for a normal interview. Suddenly, she was talking about things I'd never told *anybody:* my sister, my grandmother's coconut cake. I was shocked. How did she know all these things about me? Who told her? I had to remind myself, Oh, yeah, it's in the book. It's all in the book.

I felt so exposed, so out-there during that interview. As we spoke, though, I slowly came to realize that what was exposed was just me. The real me. Not this image I'd built up over the years to hide behind, this wall of little secrets, one brick after another, but *me*. And suddenly the interview became easy. Almost healing. Because I didn't have to deal with the wall anymore; I didn't have to hide anything from anyone. I'd already talked about it all in the book and it was right there for anyone to see.

Had I not written this book, my new album and tour would have been weighed down with the breakup of my relationship. Everyone would have been asking the same questions over and over. In the same way that "outing" David as my children's father stopped the barrage of questions and jokes on the subject, this book enabled me to stand up and get on with my life without staying focused on the past, on the personal. There was no more huge question mark as to what had happened, why it had happened, how it had happened. Instead of being forced into my past, reliving the same questions and problems over and over again with every new interviewer, I could just point to the book. Smile and tell them that the answers to all their questions were right there.

The reaction to the book was really gratifying. *The New York Times* bestseller list. Wow. All of my friends were really supportive, even the ones who felt a little left out because they hadn't really known the depth of the problems between Julie and me. The funny thing is, people always ask me about my sister, about my relationship with her. They think it was sort of left hanging in the book, and they always ask to get some sort of resolution about it. But there isn't any resolution. It's left hanging in the book because it's left hanging in life. We traded messages just as the book was coming out, when I'd heard that someone from one of the newsmagazines had called her and I wanted to apologize. After all, she didn't ask for this attention, this intrusion into her life. But we never spoke face-to-face, either about the book or the issues. Like I say . . . it's still hanging there.

My mother, on the other hand, made it very clear what she thought of the book. She felt it was shameful of me to put my dirty laundry, my family's private matters, out there for everyone to look at. Though our love for each other isn't in question, I think she's still angry at me about that. About the impropriety of talking about "secrets" out loud.

But I'm keeping true to that idea. The idea that the only shame is in hiding something, in not letting it see the light of day. I've had to deal with that so much this past year when I talk to my children. About the breakup. About how they have two mommies who love them. In two different houses. For Beckett, this past year is when he really became conscious, so this life is all he knows. Bailey, though, remembers how life was before, when Julie and I lived together. Bailey spent the first half of this year talking about going back to the old house, to the old life. And I'd have long conversations with her, helping her formulate the idea that just because things are different doesn't mean she's loved any less. She might not understand it all yet, but she feels loved by everyone in both houses, and, at the end of the day, that's what's important.

It helps that Bailey can see me with another woman, that she can see me happy in a relationship rather than sad. Excited rather than worried. That she can see a couple who spend more time loving each other than fighting.

Oh, I didn't mention that, did I? My new relationship. It's funny—just when I thought things were at their worst, when I'd finally adjusted to life alone, someone stepped into my life and opened all those doors that I'd just been looking at, too scared to open them.

After those weeks alone in my house, I tried to go out again, to date. And I found myself instantly falling back into the same old patterns. Everyone I wanted, was attracted to, wasn't available to me for one reason or another. But those are the people I'm drawn to, the ones I can't have. After the book and the breakup, though, I really saw those patterns for what they were. And now that I was out in the nightmarish dating world again, those patterns were so obvious that it was like someone slapping me on the forehead.

I was really struggling with all this when I went out one night with my friend Kathy Najimy to a ladies' bar in West Hollywood called Felt. Kathy's sort of my partner in crime, she's the most lesbian-friendly woman I know . . . all the while devoted to her husband and daughter. (Kathy! You're in the book!) When I go to a gay bar on the spur of the moment, it can be a little uncomfortable. Because suddenly I'm the power lesbian in the room and there's no place for me to go and just hang. It feels like all eyes are on me, waiting for something, expecting something. Not exactly a comfortable way to meet people. So we walked into Felt and beelined for an open table.

On the way across the room, I saw a beautiful young woman at the corner table. Short blond hair and striking, smoky eyes. But we whisked right by her. Later in the evening, I was talking to a young man who was working on the GLAAD awards, when he asked me if I wanted to meet his friend Tammy. "She's an actress," he said. "On the WB show, *Popular*," I shrugged. Sure.

And then she walks across the room toward us. That woman with the eyes. She sat down next to me and we started talking. I don't know that we've stopped yet. Tammy wasn't a fan. She wasn't that interested in who I was. She was interested in me. Just me. "I hope you don't have a problem with age," she said, "because I'm twenty-six . . . but I'd love to take you out to dinner." Right there she asked me out on a date. Now, I don't think I've been asked on a date in forever, and here was this beautiful twenty-six-year-old wanting to take me to dinner. Needless to say, I was charmed. She gave me her phone number and said I should call her to take her up on it.

It took me a full week to call. After all, here's a beautiful woman who wants me to call her. There must be something wrong, right? It took me that long to realize that I had a choice. That I could fall back into my old pattern of falling for unavailable women, live that old life all over again. Or I could move forward, doing my best to break the chains of habit. I didn't know anything about this woman other than the fact that she was gay, available, and attracted to me. So I picked up the phone and I called.

Tammy took me to dinner. And it was great. I was very open and honest about where I was in my life, what was happening with me, and she met me tit for tat. She said, okay you've got your stuff; here's mine. And we talked, honestly, emotionally, about who we were and what we wanted. It was a foundation built with honesty, something I've never really experienced before.

Loving Tammy is, in many ways, a real acceptance of who I am as a gay woman. Just like me, she's always known she's gay. And has struggled with it. And come to terms with it. Her sexuality isn't an issue for her, it just *is*. Our relationship continues to grow and deepen to this day. And I believe that it's because it's built on trust, on an honest acceptance of who each of us really is as an individual.

What's also been powerful this year is my rediscovery of myself as a solo performer. That's how I started, down in the bars in Long Beach, and every step on the road to success and fame has been a step away from that. Things got bigger, and louder, and just . . . more. So just around the time the book came out, I was thinking that making *Skin* had been such a solo process that maybe I should go *on tour* solo. Everyone thought it was a great idea. But I instantly had second thoughts. I was terrified. I thought I was gonna get up there, play four songs, and have everyone be bored to tears.

But the tour's been fabulous. Maybe one of my best ever. It's just me up there on stage. No filter, no band. Nothing to get between me and the audience. There's an intimacy that comes with being alone on stage. An intimacy and a real sense of freedom. I can do anything I want, play anything I want. Switch the song list midset. Have a shot of tequila. Anything.

It feels like going back to where I started. Back to the bars. Sure, its a *huge* bar. But it's still just me and an audience. And a stage—which remains my favorite place in the world.

For so many years my professional life was so separate from my family life. Now, for the first time, I'm beginning to feel like they're two sides of the same coin. If I can be the same person on stage that I am at home with my kids, that I am with Tammy, then I'll have really found a way to bring everything together. It's all about becoming whole. I might not be there yet, but at least the path is clear.

Life remains an open book. But the great part is . . . I still get to fill in all the blank pages.

Song Lyric Credits

...